1001

Smartest Things
TEACHERS
EVER SAID

Edited and with an Introduction by
Randy Howe

LYONS PRESS
Guilford, Connecticut
An imprint of Globe Pequot Press

To Alberto, Suzanne, and Nicole

Lyons Press in an imprint of Globe Pequot Press

Library of Congress Cataloging-in-Publication Data
Howe, Randy.
  1001 smartest things teachers ever said / Randy Howe.
    p. cm.
One thousand one smartest things teachers ever said
Includes biliographical references.
ISBN 978-1-59921-882-3
1. Teachers—Quotations. I. Title.
LB1775.H65 2010
371.102—dc22

                          2009043595

Printed in the United States of America
10 9 8 7 6 5 4 3 2 1

Contents

Introduction

Teachers are lifelong learners. They tend to be naturally curious and reflective. The best teachers present their curriculum with confidence, but unbeknownst to their students, they are constantly thinking, rethinking, and refining. In addition, the best teachers always know they can further hone their craft to build an even better mousetrap to "ensnare" the minds of their students. This book is about those teachers. It is written—literally—by those teachers. The 1,001 quotes contained herein all have something to say about a life spent working with kids.

1,001 Smartest Things Teachers Ever Said has its roots not in a classroom, but in a conference room in which a wise editor and her sage sales team decided a book like this would sell well as a gift for teachers. I agreed and quickly signed on to edit the book, more than happy to combine my two professions in one wonderful project. Together, the editors and I envisioned a scene experienced by many teachers at the end of the year or during the holidays. An appreciative student quietly approaches the teacher's desk, says "Thank you," hands the gift-wrapped package over to his or her teacher, then shuffles away. That night, the teacher unwraps the present, jots down that student's name on a "thank you card" list, and then flips through the pages before shelving the book for some later, more convenient time after the school year comes to an end.

This book has turned out to be more than that, though. Not just inspirational, it is a book that is downright informational. In fact, it isn't just a gift for a student to give to a teacher. It is a book a mentor might hand to a new teacher. It is a book a proud parent might give to a recently graduated son or daughter, getting ready to step into the classroom for the first time. It is a book that even a veteran teacher can learn from. This is because *1001 Smartest Things Teachers Ever Said* is built to teach. As it should be.

Right off the bat, there is a chapter on the art of teaching. The quotes in this first chapter of the book serve to celebrate the fact that no matter how much teachers use data and the latest research to inform their teaching, it is still a profession for the creatively inclined. Quality educators make the work look easy and know how important it is to infuse their teaching with the kind of fun and flair that gets students excited! In the second chapter, we dive deeper into the nitty-gritty. At the core of our profession is one simple goal: to build knowledge. Of course teachers are dedicated to turning students into conscientious, hard-working, ethical adults, but assessments are designed to gauge knowledge and report cards are intended to deliver the news on what has been achieved and what areas require more work. Thus, "Building Knowledge."

The third chapter is titled "The Philosophy Behind Good Teaching." Since time began, great thinkers have been pontificating on teachers and their craft. In this manner, the great thinkers themselves are teachers. That is why I included some folks who taught with their words, even though they never spent a day in a traditional classroom. In "Mastering the Craft and Managing the Classroom," the hardest aspects of the job take center stage. The nitty-gritty gets even grittier with words of wisdom about asking oneself the tough questions after a lesson or unit, about helping a school go from good to great, and about how a teacher will make the transition from needing a mentor to serving as one. The nuts and bolts advice continues with contributions about the foundation of good teaching—classroom management. Here, more than in any other chapter, *1001 Smartest Things Teachers Ever Said* shows itself to be a teaching tool and not just another bookshelf decoration. Without holding the class's attention, the teacher will find it very hard to enjoy the company of his or her students. Without a large toolbox of classroom management skills, a bad situation can quickly snowball into an awful situation. For everybody. In the end, this book should benefit the students as much as each teacher who reads it. Kids want someone they can trust at the helm; they want to know that the classroom is a calm, safe place for them to achieve their goals. Only in this kind of environment can students truly be held accountable, and that is why the next chapter is called "Advice and Accountability."

Learning is a road with twists and turns as well as the occasional pedal-to-the-metal straightaway, thus the chapter "Learning as a Process." When we learn, we are changing; not in a vacuum, but as part of a greater movement. In the classroom, a teacher issues a challenge, then another, then another. Done correctly, the challenge meets each student where he or she is, in terms of knowledge and skills. Once the student, or group of students, meets the challenge, it's time to celebrate! All sorts of challenges and celebrations are covered in "Doing It for the Kids." In addition, there are quotes that provide justification for both challenging them and celebrating them.

The chapter that follows is sure to strike a chord with all teachers. It is called "The Importance of Schools." Three cheers for that! It is hard to argue against the idea of keeping school doors open so that we may someday close down unnecessary jails. The final chapters of the book are fun and funny, educational and inspirational. "On the Lighter Side" runs the gamut of gallows humor to straight-out hilarity, and then there is "Closure to the Lesson." This is where you will find motivating quotes, so very important because just as kids need to be inspired, so do their teachers. I hope *1001 Smartest Things Teachers Ever Said* will inspire you in your work.

The e-mail programs most of us use offer the option of a signature line as a way of signing off with a little personal touch, and this is the perfect place for a favorite quote. For some time now, an important part of my signature line has been, "Nine-tenths of education is encouragement," from Nobel Prize–winning novelist Anatole France. It is the perfect message for me to send as a special education teacher. It is a little reminder to frustrated parents to stick with their child; to not give up or think that they have a "bad kid." It is also a message to teachers who don't necessarily want to put in the extra effort any more. Sometimes people get burned out on a particular student. France is telling us, though, that with encouragement, anything is possible. And rather than sending a direct statement that might put someone on the defensive, I am trying to subtly say the same. Teachers need encouragement, too.

Chances are pretty good that among the 1,001 quotes within, you will find one that represents your educational philosophy. You might also find one to help introduce your students to a new unit or assignment. Quotes have long served to plant a seed as a class switches gears from one topic to another. This also works when a reader begins a new book. In literature, a quote strategically placed between the title page and the first sentence is called an epigraph. The inscription on a statue or memorial is also called an epigraph and reflects the importance of selecting just the right words. If you're not already doing so, why not provide the kids with an epigraph? Something that sets a tone or sends a message? Not only could you place the appropriate quote at the top of a rubric or assignment sheet, you might also decorate your classroom with these appropriate quotes. You are about to read 1,001 potential epigraphs, and I'm sure that you will find most to be in accordance with your ideas about teaching, school, and children. This was my goal as I worked to put together a book that I hope will prove to be more than just a gift.

Randy Howe
August 2009

Education and the Art of Teaching

But the first day of school is our second New Year's. It is our day to make resolutions, to look backward to former lapses and triumphs and to look ahead, usually with a mix of anxiety and hope, to the year to come.

—MARK EDMUNDSON, AUTHOR

Good teachers are glad when a term begins and a little sad when it ends.

—Margaret Mead, anthropologist

The dream begins, most of the time, with a teacher who believes in you, who tugs and pushes and leads you on to the next plateau, sometimes poking you with a sharp stick called truth.

—Dan Rather, journalist

It is not a job that you can just leave on your desk
and return to the next day; you take it home with you regularly.

—*Daniel R. Kuznik, 2008 Indiana Teacher of the Year*

Have you ever really had a teacher? One who saw you as a raw
but precious thing, a jewel that, with wisdom, could be polished
to a proud shine?

—Mitch Albom, journalist

Teachers teach because they care.

—Horace Mann, educator

Teaching is a demanding career that takes a heart filled
with hope and translates that into action for every child in
a community.

—Pascale Creek Pinner,
2008 Hawaii Teacher of the Year

I swear . . . to hold my teacher in this art equal to my own parents; to make him partner in my livelihood; when he is in need of money to share mine with him; to consider his family as my own brothers and to teach them this art, if they want to learn it, without fee or indenture.

—Hippocrates, physician

In a completely rational society, the best of us would aspire to be teachers and the rest of us would have to settle for something less, because passing civilization along from one generation to the next ought to be the highest honor and highest responsibility anyone could have.

—Lee Iacocca, corporate executive

Men learn while they teach.

—Seneca, philosopher

A good teacher is never done with their preparation—grading, evaluations, planning—because they are always trying to reinvent, improve, and inspire.

—Dr. David Carlson, scientist

The most effective teacher will always be biased,
for the chief force in teaching is confidence and enthusiasm.

—Joyce Cary, writer

The man who can make hard things easy is the educator.

—Ralph Waldo Emerson, philosopher

Teachers who are passionate about their work engage students directly and relentlessly, stimulating the innate desire of children to learn.

—Anthony Mullen, 2009 National Teacher of the Year

I am a teacher. A teacher is someone who leads. There is no magic here. I do not walk on water, I do not part the sea. I just love children.

—Marva Collins, educator

I am not a teacher, but an awakener.

—Robert Frost, poet

It seems that everything we do in our lives as teachers is like a spinning spiral because we touch students, parents, colleagues and strangers, and we become more astute, more caring and better educators.

—MARILYN JACHETTI WHIRRY, 2000 NATIONAL TEACHER OF THE YEAR

Those who educate children are more to be honored than those who produce them; for these only gave them life, those the art of living well.

—Aristotle, philosopher

Better than a thousand days of diligent study is one day with a great teacher.

— *Japanese proverb*

Fifteen years after I sat on the big cozy rug in her Kindergarten classroom, Ms. Cerbone remembered my name, the bows I used to wear in my hair, the dresses that my mom made for me. Each time we ran into each other, she would recall the memories with a smile. She never forgot.

—Kimberly Buckley, 2nd grade teacher

There's no word in the language I revere more than "teacher." My heart sings when a kid refers to me as his teacher, and it always has. I've honored myself and the entire family of man by becoming a teacher.

—PAT CONROY, AUTHOR

Helping young people find their way in the world is one of the greatest contributions a teacher can make.

—Jennifer J. Montgomery, 2003 North Dakota Teacher of the Year

Rosie, an autistic child, talks to me now and can say her name. Possibly she could have reached these milestones in another classroom, but it happened in mine. What greater joy can a teacher feel than to witness a child's successes?

—*Michelle L. Graham, kindergarten and 1st grade teacher*

A teacher's mind-sets, skills, and actions are the most influential tool in sculpting the mind-sets, skills, and actions of students.

—Kristin Bourguet, 2007 Arizona Teacher of the Year

For many students, their teachers may be the only adult with whom they have a meaningful conversation all day.

—Vickie Gill, educator

We cannot enter a learning society, an education age,
without giving teachers the recognition they deserve.
—Federico Mayor, Director-General of UNESCO

Those who trust us educate us.

—George Eliot (Mary Ann Evans), author

Teaching allows me to be an important part of so many lives,
to touch a future I'll never see, to make a difference.
I can't imagine any other career.

—Mary Schlieder, 2008 Nebraska Teacher of the Year

The task of the excellent teacher is to stimulate "apparently ordinary"
people to unusual effort. The tough problem is not in identifying
winners: it is in making winners out of ordinary people.

—K. Patricia Cross, educator

If you would thoroughly know anything, teach it to others.

—TRYON EDWARDS, THEOLOGIAN

Good teachers are costly, but bad teachers cost more.

—Bob Talbert, writer

No printed word, nor spoken plea can teach young minds what they should be. Not all the books on all the shelves— but what the teachers are themselves.

—Rudyard Kipling, writer

A high-school teacher, after all, is a person deputized by the rest of us to explain to the young what sort of world they are living in, and to defend, if possible, the part their elders are playing in it.

—Emile Capouya, writer

What the teacher is, is more important than what he teaches.

—Karl Menninger, psychiatrist

The whole concept of celebrity pisses me off. While I'm not a celebrity, it's such a weird concept that society has cooked up for us. Astronauts and teachers are much more amazing than actors.

—Joseph Gordon-Levitt, actor

I am a teacher first, music is my curriculum.

—ANDREA PETERSON, 2007 WASHINGTON TEACHER OF THE YEAR

As educators, we sometimes are a little shy about tooting our own horn. We have done so much with so little for so long, we're afraid that they'll expect us to do everything with nothing.

—*Hal W. Adams, 2008 Utah Teacher of the Year*

In our world of big names, curiously, our true heroes tend to be anonymous. In this life of illusion and quasi-illusion, the person of solid virtues who can be admired for something more substantial than his well-knownness often proves to be the unsung hero: the teacher, the nurse, the mother, the honest cop, the hard worker at lonely, underpaid, unglamorous, unpublicized jobs.

—Daniel J. Boorstin, writer

As a child, I taught my dolls, my dogs, and the kids next door. I never wavered in my desires and determination to become not just a teacher, but a really good teacher who made memories in the minds of children.

—Sharon M. Draper, 1997 National Teacher of the Year

The teacher is the chief learner in the classroom.

—Donald Graves, researcher

With everything I've seen, I think I've come up with the key to successful education in America. . . . It has everything to do with teachers.

—Ron Clark, 2001 Disney National Teacher of the Year

The best teachers I ever had were science teachers... thus my chosen profession! They were great because they loved their subject matter as much as I did and they inspired me to pursue my questions, curiosities, and interests. They were active, life-long learners and that rubbed off on me.

—*Jim Gardineer, science teacher*

Teaching is the best way I know of regaining balance in your egocentric outlook on life.

—Barbara Gasparik, child development teacher

I still felt the responsibility 24 hours a day!
Teaching wasn't only my job, it was fast becoming my lifestyle.

—Scott D. Niemann, 3rd and 4th grade teacher

I cannot join the space program and restart my life as an astronaut, but this opportunity to connect my abilities as an educator with my interests in history and space is a unique opportunity to fulfill my early fantasies.

—Christa McAuliffe, astronaut

I still can not get used to how much my heart soars with every student's success, and how a piece of my heart is plucked away when any student slips away.

—DELISSA L. MAI, 9TH GRADE TEACHER

The true teacher defends his pupils against his own personal influence.

—Amos Bronson Alcott, writer

People snicker, "Those who can't do, teach." But, oh, how right they are. I could never, ever do all I dream of doing. I could never ever be an opera star, a baseball umpire... a great lover, a great liar, a trapeze artist, a writer, a dancer... or a thousand other aspirations I have had, while having only been given one thin ticket in this lottery of life!

—Esmé Raji Codell, educator

A good professor is a bastard perverse enough to think what he thinks is important, not what government thinks is important.

—*Edward C. Banfield, writer*

You can't stop a teacher when they want to do something. They just do it.

—J. D. Salinger, author

Most of us end up with no more than five or six people who remember us. Teachers have thousands of people who remember them for the rest of their lives.

—ANDREW A. ROONEY, COMMENTATOR

I owe a lot to my teachers and mean to pay them back someday.

—Stephen Leacock, writer

The good teacher makes the poor student good and the good student superior. When our students fail, we, as teachers, too, have failed.

—Marva Collins, educator

I am quite sure that in the hereafter she will take me by the hand and lead me to my proper seat.

—Bernard Baruch, financier

The invention of IQ did a great disservice to creativity in education… Individuality, personality, originality, are too precious to be meddled with by amateur psychiatrists whose patterns for a "wholesome personality" are inevitably their own.

—Joel H. Hildebrand, scientist

The fragrance always stays in the hand that gives the rose.

—HADA BEJAR, WRITER

Diligence is a great teacher.

—*Proverb*

We all understand service for pay or even praise, but only a small number understand selfless service as it relates to the good of the whole.

—*G. G. Dewey, writer*

What nobler employment, or more valuable to the state, than that of the man who instructs the rising generation.

—Marcus Tullius Cicero, philosopher

Be an opener of doors for such as come after thee.
—Ralph Waldo Emerson, philosopher

I needed to give. My vocation needed to have deeper meaning, to have relationship, to have heart. I needed to teach.

—Michael Geisen, 2008 National Teacher of the Year

Who dares to teach, must never cease to learn.

—John Cotton Dana, librarian

Teachers are the providers of truth and opportunity.

—Pascale Creek Pinner, 2008 Hawaii Teacher of the Year

Teachers, I believe, are the most responsible and important members of society because their professional efforts affect the fate of the earth.

—HELEN CALDICOTT, PEACE ACTIVIST

Teachers are more than any other class the guardians of civilization.

—*Bertrand Russell, philosopher*

Strong, enthusiastic, powerful teaching has more impact on student learning than any other factor. Because of that, top teaching will always be the biggest key to student achievement.

—Jennifer J. Montgomery, 2003 North Dakota Teacher of the Year

Behold, I do not give lectures or a little charity,
When I give I give myself.

—*Walt Whitman, poet*

The great teacher is not the man who supplies the most facts,
but the one in whose presence we become different people.
—Ralph Waldo Emerson, philosopher

It is written that he who governs well, leads the blind; but that he
who teaches, gives them eyes.

—David O. McKay, religious leader

We make the road, others will make the journey.
—Victor Hugo, author

Teachers must be celebrated for moving civilization from
ignorance to enlightenment, from apathy to responsibility.
—Sharon M. Draper, 1997 National Teacher of the Year

The best teacher is the one who suggests rather than dogmatizes, and inspires his listener with the wish to teach himself.

—Edward Bulwer-Lytton, writer

The professional teacher must move beyond existing models of educational theory and philosophy and become an artist and a creator.

—Anthony Mullen, 2009 National Teacher of the Year

A good teacher is a master of simplification and an enemy of simplism.

—LOUIS A. BERMAN, MUSICIAN

Teaching gives me a greater sense of my own humanity.

—Camille Banks-Lee, English teacher

If I had to do it over again, I would still become a teacher. Teaching is hard work, but its personal rewards are priceless.

—*Thomas A. Fleming, 1992 National Teacher of the Year*

A teacher who is attempting to teach without inspiring the pupil with a desire to learn is hammering on a cold iron.

—*Horace Mann, educator*

One can lead a horse to water but he will drink only if he is thirsty and believes that the water is safe.

—George Edwin Goodfellow, 2008 Rhode Island Teacher of the Year

In teaching, it is the method and not the content that is the message... the drawing out, not the pumping in.

—Ashley Montague, anthropologist

Teaching is an instinctual art, mindful of potential, craving of realizations, a pausing, seamless process.

—*A. Bartlett Giamatti, educator*

Education is the art of making man ethical.
—*Georg Hegel, philosopher*

Learning time is precious and the deepest, most meaningful learning occurs when students have the opportunity to be creative with the concepts or material.

—Susanne H. Frensley, 2007 Tennessee Teacher of the Year

Each experience that I plan for my students should have three key elements: significance, joy, and celebration. I know I can't achieve these elements in every lesson, but it is my driving goal.

—Margaret Holtschlag, 2000 Michigan Teacher of the Year

Good teaching is primarily an art, and can neither be defined or standardized... Good teachers are born and made; neither part of the process can be omitted.

—Joel H. Hildebrand, scientist

Good teaching is one-fourth preparation and three-fourths theatre.

—Gail Godwin, writer

People learn more quickly by doing something or seeing something done.

—Gilbert Highet, writer

Creativity does not exist on a continuum. Rather, there are small groups of teachers in every school that work in unique systems.

—JIM SCHULZ, 2000 DISNEY TEACHER OF THE YEAR

I'm not trying to create a spark—I'm trying to start an out-of-control forest fire of learning.

—Eric Langhorst, 2008 Missouri Teacher of the Year

It is the supreme art of the teacher to awaken joy in creative expression and knowledge.

—Albert Einstein, physicist

Creative activity is not a superimposed, extraneous task against which the body or brain protests, but an orchestration of... joyful doing.

—Gyorgy Kepes, artist

If my students do not feel my passion to teach, I have failed as a teacher.

—Anthony Mullen,
2009 National Teacher of the Year

Expand our creative repertoires so that we have many tricks in our bag.

—LAUREN K. AYERS, PSYCHOLOGIST

In my classroom, the students never know what is up my sleeve.

—Melanie Teemant, 2007 Nevada Teacher of the Year

I want to instill in my students the desire to explore, to create, and to learn. I want to actively involve them in their education and get them excited about learning.

—Charlotte Mohling, 2007 South Dakota Teacher of the Year

Passersby in the hallway usually hear us learning well before they see us learning!

—Joshua M. Anderson, 2007 Kansas Teacher of the Year

Hope and its twin, possibility, best describe the art of teaching

—Camille Banks-Lee, English teacher

You have to vary how you teach things to kids. You need to have that ability to stand up, move around, sing, dance. That's important.

—Pascale Creek Pinner, 2008 Hawaii Teacher of the Year

The art of teaching is the art of assisting discovery.

—Mark Van Doren, poet

Teaching is a creative endeavor
and I believe it's OK to color outside the lines.

—Michele Forman, 2001 National Teacher of the Year

To know how to suggest is the art of teaching.

—Henri-Frederic Amiel, philosopher

A performer needs an audience, just as an audience needs a performance, and this relationship is equally applicable to teachers and students.

—Seth Berg, 2008 Colorado Teacher of the Year

The only way I can explain the profession to the nonteachers in my life is by using the analogy that it is like putting on a different Broadway show every day.

—Lewis Chappelear, 2008 California Teacher of the Year

Even the most experienced and accomplished teachers are often quite insecure about their craft. This is because teaching is an art that is never mastered, because there is always room for improvement in even the most polished lesson.

—Gary Bloom and Barbara Davis, educators

You must prove matters from your own experience.

—J.J. Dewey, writer

I offer my students as many ideas as I can by showing them through literature that there is nothing that has not already been felt, experienced or thought; but much to be discovered in a new way.

—Janis T. Gabay, 1990 National Teacher of the Year

Content rigor occurs after content inspiration.

—George Edwin Goodfellow, 2008 Rhode Island Teacher of the Year

Learning is a natural behavior. It's just a matter of doing what you can to bring it out.

—Melissa Bartlett, 2003 North Carolina Teacher of the Year

I touch the future. I teach.

—*Christa McAuliffe, author*

Building Knowledge

The basic idea behind teaching is to teach people what they need to know.

—Carl Rogers, psychologist

Education's purpose is to replace an empty mind with an open one.

—Malcom S. Forbes, publisher

Knowledge exists to be imparted.

—Ralph Waldo Emerson, philosopher

If knowledge can create problems, it is not through ignorance that we can solve them.

—Isaac Asimov, writer

And what, Socrates, is the food of the soul? Surely, I said, knowledge is the food of the soul.

— Plato, philosopher

The aim of education is the knowledge, not of facts, but of values.

—William Ralph Inge, playwright

The highest function of the teacher consists not so much in imparting knowledge as in stimulating the pupil in its love and pursuit.

—Anonymous

If a man empties his purse into his head, no man can take it away from him. An investment in knowledge always pays the best interest.

—Benjamin Franklin, author and printer

Knowledge is the antidote to fear.

—*Ralph Waldo Emerson, philosopher*

The Great Society is a place where every child can find knowledge to enrich his mind and to enlarge his talents... It is a place where men are more concerned with the quality of their goals than the quantity of their goods.

—President Lyndon B. Johnson

Seek knowledge from the cradle to the grave.

—Muhammad, theologian

Knowledge is of two kinds. We know a subject ourselves, or we know where we can find information upon it.

—Samuel Johnson, author

Wealth, if you use it, comes to an end; learning, if you use it, increases.

—Swahili saying

As our knowledge is converted to wisdom, the door to opportunity is unlocked.

—*Barbara W. Winder, religious leader*

Today our knowledge of the past is increasing at an unprecedented rate, and this at both ends of its ever lengthening vista. The archaeologists are making history by exhuming buried and forgotten civilizations as fast as the politicians are making it by taking new action for contemporary historians to study.

—Arnold J. Toynbee, historian

Everything you see is the direct result of teachers spreading knowledge to vast amounts of people.

—*Anthony Mullen, 2009 National Teacher of the Year*

It is not the answer that enlightens, but the question.

—Eugene Ionesco, playwright

The very concept of history implies the scholar and the reader. Without a generation of civilized people to study history, to preserve its records, to absorb its lessons and relate them to its own problems, history, too, would lose its meaning.

—GEORGE F. KENNAN, POLITICAL SCIENTIST

History not used is nothing, for all intellectual life is action, like practical life, and if you don't use the stuff—well, it might as well be dead.

—*Arnold J. Toynbee, historian*

Every man has a right to be wrong in his opinions, but no man has a right to be wrong in his facts.

—Bernard Baruch, financier

The utmost extent of man's knowledge is to know that he knows nothing.

—Joseph Addison, writer

Genius, when young, is divine.

—Prime Minister Benjamin Disraeli

Education is not merely a means for earning a living or an instrument for the acquisition of wealth. It is an initiation into life of spirit, a training of the human soul in the pursuit of truth and the practice of virtue.

—Vijaya Lakshmi Pandit

What sculpture is to a block of marble, education is to a human soul.

—JOSEPH ADDISON, WRITER

We will conserve only what we love. We will love only what we understand. We will understand only what we are taught.

—Anonymous

A man should first direct himself in the way he should go. Only then should he instruct others.

—**Buddha**

We live in a time of such rapid change and growth of knowledge that only he who is in a fundamental sense a scholar—that is, a person who continues to learn and inquire—can hope to keep pace, let alone play the role of guide.

—Nathan M. Pusey, educator

To waken interest and kindle enthusiasm is the sure way to teach easily and successfully.

—Tryon Edwards, theologian

Reading is to the mind, what exercise is to the body.
— *Sir Richard Steele, writer*

Always to see the general in the particular is the very foundation of genius.

—Arthur Schopenhauer, philosopher

I try to maintain a mixture of quiet patience, boisterous enthusiasm, and positive outlook, holding the belief that attitude can be just as contagious as the colds notoriously spread throughout elementary schools.

—Tamra A. Tiong, 2007 New Mexico Teacher of the Year

My job is to teach, but my passion is setting students' minds ablaze with a love of creative learning and the power of knowledge.

—*Keil E. Hileman, 2004 Kansas Teacher of the Year*

Teaching is a calling, not a choice.
— Mary Ann Alexander, cosmetology teacher

We are here to help students develop skills that will carry them into another century, which promises to be no less revolutionary than the Industrial Revolution of the late eighteenth and early nineteenth centuries.

—MARY BETH BLEGEN, 1996 NATIONAL TEACHER OF THE YEAR

The one exclusive sign of thorough knowledge is
the power of teaching.

—Aristotle, philosopher

A good teacher needs not only a good understanding of what he or she teaches, but also a sense of excitement in learning and a clear vision of how the key elements of a subject can be conveyed to students.

—Michele Forman, 2001 National Teacher of the Year

Education is the jewel casting brilliance into the future.

—Mari Evans, writer

Genius without education is like silver in the mine.

—*Benjamin Franklin, author and printer*

We teachers must envision success for our students so strongly that the vision becomes contagious and our students catch it and refuse to ever let it go.

—Tamara Steen, 2005 Washington Teacher of the Year

If you think education is expensive, try ignorance.

—*Derek Bok, educator*

Life is an exciting business, and most exciting when it is lived for others.

—Helen Keller, author and lecturer

Blessed is the influence of one true, loving human soul on another.

—GEORGE ELIOT (MARY ANN EVANS), AUTHOR

To me the sole hope of human salvation lies in teaching.

—George Bernard Shaw, playwright

Teaching is the world's most important job.

—UNESCO (United Nations Educational, Scientific and Cultural Organization)

Teaching is the essential profession, the one that makes all other professions possible.

—Jason Scott Fulmer,
2004 South Carolina Teacher of the Year

A human being is not attaining his full heights until he is educated.

—HORACE MANN, EDUCATOR

An educated man... is thoroughly inoculated against humbug, thinks for himself and tries to give his thoughts, in speech or on paper, some style.

—Alan Simpson, educator

We can get over being poor, but it takes longer to get over being ignorant.

—Jane Sequichie Hifler, writer

Education is a specifically human activity. Unlike other animals, man inherits something over and above what is transmitted to him automatically by physical and psychic heredity.

—Arnold J. Toynbee, historian

Every day is a symphony of rigor, relevance, and relationships inside and outside my classroom.

—Lewis Chappelear, 2008 California Teacher of the Year

Education is not a preparation for life; education is life itself.

—John Dewey, educational philosopher

We are born weak, we have need of help; we are born destitute of everything, we stand in need of assistance; we are born stupid, we have need of understanding. All that we are not possessed of at our birth, and which we require when we grow up, is bestowed on us by education.

—JEAN JACQUES ROUSSEAU, PHILOSOPHER

The educated differ from the uneducated as much as the living from the dead.

—ARISTOTLE, PHILOSOPHER

Awareness need never remain superficial in an educated man, whereas unawareness is certain to be ignorance probably compounded by arrogance.

—National Conference on Higher Education (1964)

The whole object of education is . . . to develop the mind. The mind should be a thing that works.

—Sherwood Anderson, author

Let us think of education as the means of developing our greatest abilities, because in each of us there is a private hope and dream which, fulfilled, can be translated into benefit for everyone and greater strength for our nation.

—President John F. Kennedy

Our best chance for happiness is education.

—Mark Van Doren, poet

There is no education like adversity.

—Prime Minister Benjamin Disraeli

Education is light, lack of it darkness.

—Russian proverb

An age is called Dark not because the light fails to shine, but because people refuse to see it.

—James A. Michener, author

Education is the mother and the father.

—Motto of the "Lost Boys of the Southern Sudan"

Not to know is bad; not to wish to know is worse.

—African proverb

Remember, the future of every young man or woman you meet is not your responsibility alone. You will play your part, and what you teach, day by day, semester by semester, with all the clarity and passion you can summon, will contribute to, but not determine, the outcome of their lives.

—Thomas A. Fleming, 1992 National Teacher of the Year

The fortune of our lives therefore depends on employing well the short period of our youth.

—President Thomas Jefferson

Knowing is the measure of the man. By how much we know, so much we are.

—Ralph Waldo Emerson, philosopher

By the worldly standards of public life, all scholars in their work are of course oddly virtuous.

—Jacob Bronowski, scientist and mathematician

Unobstructed access to facts can produce unlimited good only if it is matched by the desire and ability to find out what they mean and where they lead.

—Norman Cousins, writer

What one doesn't understand one doesn't possess.

—*Johann Wolfgang von Goethe, philosopher*

What office is there which involves more responsibility, which requires more qualifications, and which ought, therefore, to be more honorable, that than of teaching?

—Harriet Martineau, journalist and feminist

A liberal education is at the heart of a civil society, and at the heart of a liberal education is the act of teaching.

—A. Bartlett Giamatti, educator

Aptitudes are assumed, they should become accomplishments. That is the purpose of all education.

—*Johann Wolfgang von Goethe, philosopher,* Elective Affinities *(1809)*

The critical factor is not class size but rather the nature of the teaching as it affects learning.

—C. B. Neblette, photographer

I believe that every human soul is teaching something to someone nearly every minute here in mortality.

—M. Russell Ballard, theologian

The first duty of a lecturer is to hand you after an hour's discourse a nugget of pure truth to wrap up between the pages of your notebooks and keep on the mantelpiece forever.

—Virginia Woolf, writer

I think, therefore I am.

—René Descartes, philosopher

Most subjects at universities are taught for no other purpose than that they may be re-taught when the students become teachers.

—Georg C. Lichtenberg, educator

Tis education forms the common mind/Just as the twig is bent, the tree's inclined.

—Alexander Pope, poet

Benevolence alone will not make a teacher, nor will learning alone do it. The gift of teaching is a peculiar talent, and implies a need and a craving in the teacher himself.

—John Jay Chapman, writer

I try to remember each day that what I teach is not as important as how I teach or who I teach.

—Melanie Teemant, 2007 Nevada Teacher of the Year

In teaching others we teach ourselves.

—*Proverb*

I teach. It's what I do. And I'm not done yet. I don't think I'll ever be.

—George Edwin Goodfellow, 2008 Rhode Island Teacher of the Year

The teaching goes on.

—*Mitch Albom, writer*

The Philosophy Behind Good Teaching

Every day I have the opportunity to model my philosophy in my own actions.

—Melanie Teemant, 2007 Nevada Teacher of the Year

Instead of alcohol and drug counselors and educators asking, "What are you doing?" we need to ask, "How are you doing?" That could almost be a philosophy unto itself. How are you doing?

—Mary Beth Blegen, 1996 National Teacher of the Year

These children taught me a very simple but often overlooked principle. Believe in a child's power to succeed and they will succeed.

—Maggie Keyser, 1999 Disney Teacher of the Year

Awaken people's curiosity. It is enough to open minds, do not overload them. Put there just a spark.

—Anatole France, author

Everything should be made as simple as possible, but not simpler.

—Albert Einstein, physicist

I thought the best teachers were the ones who could cram as much knowledge into students' heads as possible. Quickly, I discovered that the secret is to engage students so they leave your classroom asking even more questions.

—Eric Langhorst, 2008 Missouri Teacher of the Year

The teacher gives not of his wisdom,
but rather of his faith and lovingness.
—Kahlil Gibran, writer

I entered the classroom with the conviction that it was crucial for me and every other student to be an active participant, not a passive consumer . . . education that connects the will to know with the will to become.

—bell hooks (Gloria Watkins), writer and feminist

Education should turn out the pupil with something he knows well and something he can do well.
—Alfred North Whitehead, philosopher and mathematician

By learning you will teach; by teaching you will understand.

—Latin proverb

If you wish to build a ship, do not give directions and technical advice to others. Rather, show them the wonder and adventure of the open ocean.

—George Edwin Goodfellow, 2008 Rhode Island Teacher of the Year

The teacher must derive not only the capacity, but the desire, to observe natural phenomena. In our system, she must become a passive, much more than an active, influence, and her passivity shall be composed of anxious scientific curiosity and of absolute respect for the phenomenon which she wishes to observe.

—Maria Montessori, educator

Teachers open the door, but you enter by yourself.

—Chinese proverb

I believe the deepest learning occurs when students have a reason to apply knowledge and skills to real-life situations.

— Kim Schaefer, 2007 Utah Teacher of the Year

Teaching is the highest form of understanding.

—Aristotle, philosopher

I believe the teacher must embrace the whole child in a caring and positive manner for learning to occur.

> —**Betsy Rogers, 2003 National Teacher of the Year**

At present there are differences of opinion . . . for all peoples do not agree as to the things that the young ought to learn, either with a view to virtue or with a view to the best life, nor is it clear whether their studies should be regulated more with regard to intellect or with regard to character.

> —ARISTOTLE, PHILOSOPHER

One looks back with appreciation to the brilliant teachers, but with gratitude to those who touched our human feelings.

> —Carl Jung, psychologist

I believe that education is a process of living and not a preparation for future living.

> —*John Dewey, educational philosopher*

Teaching is an exhausting job. I did not, however, expect to be emotionally exhausted. I suppose the easiest way out of this dilemma would be to make myself emotionally unavailable to my students . . . Not this teacher. This teacher can't help but share in some of those emotional moments. I can't turn off a portion of myself when I walk into the classroom. It's either the whole Mrs. Baer or nothing.

—ALLISON L. BAER, 4TH TO 6TH GRADE TEACHER

Let's focus less on a "one size fits all" approach to teaching and more on "one student at a time" teaching.

—*Thomas R. Smigiel Jr., 2008 Virginia Teacher of the Year*

Certain subjects yield a general power that may be applied in any direction and should be studied by all.

—*John Locke, philosopher*

It has always seemed strange to me that in our endless discussions about education so little stress is laid on the pleasure of becoming an educated person, the enormous interest it adds to life. To be able to be caught up into the world of thought—that is to be educated.

—Edith Hamilton, educator

In my classroom, the most dominant element of my philosophy is to meet each student at his or her own level and move forward.

—Brittany E. Ray, 2007 Maine Teacher of the Year

To educate a man in mind and not in morals is to educate a menace to society.

—*President Theodore Roosevelt*

An education that does not strive to promote the fullest and most thorough understanding of the world is not worthy of the name.

—George S. Counts, educator

The important thing is not so much that every child should be taught, as that every child should be given the wish to learn.

—*John Lubbock, politician*

You cannot teach a man anything; you can only help him find it within himself.

—*Galileo Galilei, physicist*

The teacher who is indeed wise/Does not bid you to enter the house of his wisdom/But rather leads you to the threshold of your mind.

—Kahlil Gibran, writer

A great teacher never strives to explain his vision. He simply invites you to stand beside him and see for yourself.

—R. INMAN, THEOLOGIAN

If you can't explain it simply, you don't understand it well enough.

—Albert Einstein, physicist

There is humane aggression in being a great teacher, as well as genuine love.

—Mark Edmundson, author

The aim of education should be to teach us rather how to think, than what to think—rather to improve our minds, so as to enable us to think for ourselves, than to load the memory with the thoughts of other men.

—JOHN DEWEY, EDUCATIONAL PHILOSOPHER

Direct the attention of your pupil to the phenomena of nature, and you will soon awaken his curiosity; but to keep that curiosity alive, you must be in no haste to satisfy it: he should not learn but invent the sciences.

—Jean Jacques Rousseau, philosopher

A master can tell you what he expects of you. A teacher, though, awakens your own expectations.

—Patricia Neal, actress

A sufficient experimental training was believed to have been provided as long as the student had been introduced to the results of past experiments or had been allowed to watch demonstration experiments conducted by his teacher, as though it were possible to sit in rows on a wharf and learn to swim merely by watching grown-up swimmers in the water.

—Jean Piaget, child psychologist

A teacher is one who makes himself progressively unnecessary.

—Thomas Carruthers, writer

By viewing the old we learn the new.

—Chinese proverb

The real difficulty, the difficulty which has baffled the sages of all times, is rather this: how can we make our teaching so potent in the motional life of man, that its influence should withstand the pressure of the elemental psychic forces in the individual?

—ALBERT EINSTEIN, PHYSICIST

Knowledge can only be got in one way, the way of experience; there is no other way to know.

—Swami Vivekananda, spiritual leader of Vedanta philosophy

An education isn't how much you have committed to memory, or even how much you know. It's being able to differentiate between what you do know and what you don't.

—Anatole France, author

What we learn with pleasure we never forget.

—Alfred Mercier, author

To be conscious that we are perceiving and thinking is to be conscious of our own existence.

—Aristotle, philosopher

To be a teacher in the right sense is to be a learner. I am not a teacher, only a fellow student.

—Soren Kierkegaard, philosopher

The teacher's task is not to implant facts but to place the subject to be learned in front of the learner and, through sympathy, emotion, imagination and patience, to awaken in the learner the restless drive for answers and insights which enlarge the personal life and give it meaning.

—NATHAN M. PUSEY, EDUCATOR

The most important function of education at any level is to develop the personality of the individual and the significance of his life to himself and to others. This is the basic architecture of a life; the rest is ornamentation and decoration of the structure.

—Grayson Kirk, educator

Good teaching is more a giving of right questions than a giving of right answers.

—Josef Albers, artist

Education is not the piling on of learning, information, data, facts, skills, or abilities—that's training or instruction—but is rather a making visible what is hidden as a seed.

—*Thomas Moore, poet and entertainer*

But this bridge will only take you halfway there—The last few steps you'll have to take alone.

—Shel Silverstein, author and illustrator

I continually strive to develop teaching methods that will fit the needs of my students' learning styles while maintaining a level of teaching that does not bore more gifted students.

—Lee J. James, 2007 Mississippi Teacher of the Year

Whatever you want to teach, be brief.

—*Horace, poet*

Become a teacher with a heart:

H—help others,

E—encourage others,

A—an attitude that is positive and contagious,

R—reach out to the hurting and lonely,

T—teach others/mentor others.

—Samuel R. Bennett, 2006 Florida Teacher of the Year

Teaching is truth mediated by personality.

—Phyllis Brooks, actress

Good teachers are those who know how little they know. Bad teachers are those who think they know more than they don't know.

—R. Verdi

To teach successfully we must tell all we know, but only what is adaptable to the student.

—Frédéric-César de La Harpe, politician

I believe that it is my job as a teacher to enable students to both expand the range of options open to them and to choose among those options.

—Justin Minkel, 2007 Arkansas Teacher of the Year

I make it a goal to greet students each day as they enter, call them by name as often as possible, and to use humor to break down barriers of class, race, age, and ability.

—Michael Geisen, 2008 National Teacher of the Year

Great teaching is brimming with energy, excitement, and passion. It's where students are motivated, teachers are vibrant, and learning is interactive.

—Lois J. Rebich, 2007 Pennsylvania Teacher of the Year

Teachers should guide without dictating,
and participate without dominating.

—*C. B. Neblette, photographer*

Sometimes the last thing learners need is for their preferred learning style to be affirmed. Agreeing to let people learn only in a way that feels comfortable and familiar can restrict seriously their chance for development.

—STEVEN BROOKFIELD, EDUCATOR

Tell me and I forget. Show me and I remember. Involve me and I understand.

—*Chinese proverb*

If history were taught in the form of stories,
it would never be forgotten.

—*Rudyard Kipling, writer*

Thought flows in terms of stories—stories about events, stories about people, and stories about intentions and achievements. The best teachers are the best storytellers. We learn in the form of stories.

—Frank Smith, writer

My philosophy of teaching has changed. Oh, we still read and discuss and write and argue. But we talk more about the "why" and "how" of learning. The students ask more questions and I try to give fewer answers.

—Mary Beth Blegen, 1996 National Teacher of the Year

The object of teaching a child is to enable him to get along without his teacher.

—Elbert Hubbard, writer

We do not learn by inference and deduction and the application of mathematics to philosophy, but by direct intercourse and sympathy.

—Henry David Thoreau, writer and naturalist

The mediocre teacher tells. The good teacher explains. The superior teacher demonstrates. The great teacher inspires.

—William Arthur Ward, author

In order for me to be successful in the classroom, I must know my students and be willing to meet them where they are.

—Eric A. Combs, 2007 Ohio Teacher of the Year

Setting an example is not the main means of influencing another, it is the only means.

—Albert Einstein, physicist

Stories help us to celebrate life with the children we teach and offer them the dream of improving the future.

—J. Mittel Stadt, writer

One of the least discussed ways of carrying a student through a hard unit of material is to challenge him with a chance to exercise his full powers, so that he may discover the pleasure of full and effective functioning . . .

—Jerome S. Bruner, psychologist

We must beware of what I will call "inert ideas" that is to say, ideas that are merely received into the mind without being utilized or tested or thrown into fresh combinations.

—Alfred North Whitehead, philosopher and mathematician

Indeed, the exciting thing about a philosophy of education is that it is always changing and growing.

—*Brittany E. Ray, 2007 Maine Teacher of the Year*

Mastering the Craft and Managing the Classroom

As a teacher you must always find new ways of growing, and you must always strive to find new ways of helping your students grow.

—Lylee Style, English teacher

To arrive at the simple is difficult.

—Rashid Elisha

I would remind teachers of how important it is to have a life outside of teaching . . . Our students deserve happy, well-rounded, rested, and exuberant adults to teach and care for them!

—ANDY BAUMGARTNER, 1999 NATIONAL TEACHER OF THE YEAR

Lead by example and try to make each day the best possible for your students.

—Eric A. Combs, 2007 Ohio Teacher of the Year

If we teach today's students as we taught yesterday's, we rob them of tomorrow.

—John Dewey, educational philosopher

I was still learning when I taught my last class.

—Clause M. Fuess, biographer

Some people see teaching as a step in a career ladder and think if you're really good you'll definitely become a principal or a superintendent. I don't see it that way. I see teaching as a lifelong craft.

—Justin Minkel, 2007 Arkansas Teacher of the Year

Acquire new knowledge whilst thinking over the old, and you may become a teacher of others.

—Confucius, philosopher

Teaching of others teacheth the teacher.

—Anwar Fuller

A lesson plan is perfect until the children arrive.

—Jane Wardrop, educator

Time is the currency of teaching. We barter with time. Every day we make small concessions, small tradeoffs, but, in the end, we know it's going to defeat us.

—Ernest L. Boyer, educator

To teach is to learn twice.

—Joseph Joubert, writer

As an educator, I accept the responsibility of becoming a life-long learner as new ideas, new technology, and new ways to approach teaching become available.

—CARIDAD "CHARITY" ALONSO, 2007 DELAWARE TEACHER OF THE YEAR

We teachers are not unlike our students. We too are comfortably unaware of our lack of knowledge.

—Andrea Peterson, 2007 Washington Teacher of the Year

I have learned as I taught, for I feel that an active learner is the best teacher.

—Sharon M. Draper, 1997 National Teacher of the Year

The best classroom-management system is a great, engaging lesson. Take the time to plan carefully so that your students will enter your classroom every day wondering, "What exciting surprises does s/he have in store for me today?"

—Jason Kamras, 2005 National Teacher of the Year

My skills as a teacher need the same nurturing as those of the students.
— *Ina B. Bouker, 2007 Alaska Teacher of the Year*

I see the mind of the five-year-old as a volcano with two vents: destructiveness and creativeness.
— Sylvia Ashton-Warner, educator

It is important that students bring a certain ragamuffin, barefoot irreverence to their studies; they are not here to worship what is known, but to question it.
— Jacob Bronowski, scientist and mathematician

If you can't relate to kids and meet them where they are, then you are going to have a tough time getting them to respect you or follow your guidance.
— **Ron Clark, 2001 Disney National Teacher of the Year**

We are working with human beings,
and things rarely go exactly as planned.

—Susanne H. Frensley, 2007 Tennessee Teacher of the Year

School success is not predicted by a child's fund of facts or a precocious ability to read as much as by emotional and social measures; being self-assured and interested; knowing what kind of behavior is expected and how to rein in the impulse to misbehave; being able to wait, to follow directions, and to turn to teachers for help; and expressing needs while getting along with other children.

—Daniel Goleman, psychologist

I believe that I aim for the heart with my students. I help them feel better about themselves first, and then the learning can take place.

—Samuel R. Bennett, 2006 Florida Teacher of the Year

Don't set your wit against a child.

—Johnathan Swift, writer

School is a place to process mistakes.

—Anita Voelker, educator

Consider how hard it is to change yourself and you'll understand what little chance you have of trying to change others.

—Jacob Braude, jurist

Praise, like gold and diamonds, owes its value only to its scarcity.

—Samuel Johnson, author

If you have a child's heart, you have his head.

—FLIP FLIPPEN, LEADERSHIP CONSULTANT

There is no human reason why a child should not admire and emulate his teacher's ability to do sums, rather than the village bum's ability to whittle sticks and smoke cigarettes. The reason why the child does not is plain enough—the bum has put himself on an equality with him and the teacher has not.

—Floyd Dell, writer

Teaching is of more importance than urging.

—*Martin Luther, theologian*

There are many ways a teacher can positively influence student learning, including a love for books and a regard for multiple world views. But the most important thing to me is to forge an unbreakable bond with each student based on mutual respect and admiration.

—Elaine B. Griffin, 1995 National Teacher of the Year

You cannot shake hands with a clenched fist.

—Prime Minister Indira Gandhi

Students should behave because they want to—not because they have to in order to avoid punishment.

—MARVIN MARSHALL, WRITER

Children do not say what they believe. They say what works. For what they will truly believe is still in its formative stage.

—George Edwin Goodfellow, 2008 Rhode Island Teacher of the Year

It's a common tendency to project our own feelings and motivations on other people's behavior— "If this means something to me, it must mean something to them."

—Stephen R. Covey, writer

Have a heart that never hardens, and a temper that never fires, and a touch that never hurts.

—Charles Dickens, author

No matter where we go, there will always be rules. There is no way out of rules but the wrong way.

—Ina B. Bouker, 2007 Alaska Teacher of the Year

The secret of education is respecting the pupil.

—Ralph Waldo Emerson, philosopher

By understanding that school was the best place for some of my children, I became committed to making my classroom a place where students feel safe as well as creating an environment that provides joy to those with unfortunate lives.

—Betsy Rogers, 2003 National Teacher of the Year

The more you prepare outside class, the less you perspire in class. The less you perspire in class, the more you inspire the class.

—HO BOON TIONG, EDUCATOR

Students need to be prepared to enter each classroom with the attitude that they are going to learn something that day.

—Lee J. James, 2006 Mississippi Teacher of the Year

He who wrestles with us strengthens our nerves
and sharpens our skills.

—*Edward Burke, artist*

Education is the ability to listen to almost anything without losing your temper or your self-confidence.

—Robert Frost, poet

Education is a kind of continuing dialogue, and a dialogue assumes... different points of view.

—Robert M. Hutchins, educator

A wise man knows and will keep his place; but a child is ignorant of his, and therefore cannot confine himself to it. There are a thousand avenues through which he will be apt to escape; it belongs to those who have the care of his education, therefore, to prevent him; a task, by the way, which is not very easy.

—JEAN JACQUES ROUSSEAU, PHILOSOPHER

Children who are forced to eat acquire a loathing for food, and children who are forced to learn acquire a loathing for knowledge.

—Bertrand Russell, philosopher

Describing her first day back in grade school, after a long absence, a teacher said, "It was like trying to hold thirty-five corks under water at the same time."

—Mark Twain, author

School disruption comes from those children who have given up hope of trying to learn anything.

—*Albert Shanker, educator*

The powers of students sometimes sink under too great severity in correction . . . while they fear everything, they cease to attempt anything.

—Quintilian, rhetorician

All genuine education is liberating, and certainly needs freedom and discipline.

—*Regina D. Archambault, writer*

The teachers who get "burned out" are not the ones who are constantly learning, which can be exhilarating, but those who feel they must stay in control and ahead of the students at all times.

—Frank Smith, writer

Once more I would adopt the graver style—
a teacher should be sparing of his smile.

— William Cowper, poet

The old saying "Put your students in rows and do not smile until December" is indeed out of date when we must seek to build community and foster collaboration among our young people.

—Jason Scott Fulmer, 2004 South Carolina Teacher of the Year

Greet your students each day with a smile on your face. It might be the only smile they see all day.

—Lois J. Rebich, 2007 Pennsylvania Teacher of the Year

Kind words can be short and easy to speak,
but their echoes are endless.

—*Mother Teresa, 1979 Nobel Peace Prize winner*

Too often we underestimate the power of a touch, a smile,
a kind word, a listening ear, an honest compliment, or the
smallest act of caring, all of which have the potential to turn
a life around.

—LEO BUSCAGLIA, AUTHOR

*A word of encouragement during a failure is worth
more than an hour of praise after success.*

—*Anonymous*

**A decline in the extrinsic payoff requires a compensating
improvement in the intrinsic satisfaction of learning if
students are to be motivated.**

—**Henry M. Levin, educator**

If you are too strict, the kids will rebel. And if you try too hard to get them to like you, they're going to walk all over you. There has to be balance.

—Ron Clark, 2001 Disney National Teacher of the Year

Children may forget what you say, but they'll never forget how you make them feel.

—Parker J. Palmer, sociologist

You can't hold a man down without staying down with him.

—Booker T. Washington, educator

Despite the need for consequences, they are not sufficient in themselves. Discipline entails more than catching a child in the act and punishing. Far more important is nurturing his will for good.

—Johann Christoph Arnold, writer

I never reprimand a boy in the evening—darkness and a troubled mind are a poor combination.

—FRANK L. BOYDEN, EDUCATOR

Obedience is the mother of success,
and success the parent of salvation.

—Aeschylus, playwright

It takes time to persuade men to do even what is for their own good.

President Thomas Jefferson

No trace of slavery ought to mix with the studies of the freeborn man . . . No study, pursued under compulsion, remains rooted in the memory.

—Plato, philosopher

A child cannot be taught by anyone who despises him . . .

—James Baldwin, author

At school Mrs. Dickens liked Paul's picture of the sailboat better than my picture of the invisible castle. At singing time she said I sang too loud. At counting time she said I left out sixteen. Who needs sixteen? I could tell it was going to be a terrible, horrible, no good, very bad day.

—Judith Viorst, children's author

The irony of punishment is that the more you use it to control your students' behaviors, the less real influence you have over them.

—Marvin Marshall, writer

Love is at the root of all healthy discipline.

—Fred Rogers, TV personality

I do not believe that I must control children, either by conditioning them with rewards and punishments or by meeting all of their "needs."

—Ina B. Bouker, 2007 Alaska Teacher of the Year

In the true student-teacher relationship authority is only recognized because it is earned.

—J. J. Dewey, writer

I don't raise my voice to these kids; I don't humiliate these children.

—Rafe Esquith, 1992 Disney National Teacher of the Year

I would laugh more and yell less. I wouldn't make big issues out of non-issues. I would enjoy the kids more and worry about authority less.

—Dolores Curran, writer

Authority is conveyed not by assuming a controlling manner, but by active listening and by developing the ability to interpret student behavior.

—Thomas A. Fleming, 1992 National Teacher of the Year

Patience is the key to paradise.

—Armenian proverb

Remember, if punishment were effective in reducing inappropriate behavior, then there would be NO discipline problems in schools.

—*Marvin Marshall, writer*

Don't forget to emphasize the positive. There's great power in highlighting the positive behaviors and positive efforts of students.

—Jason Kamras, 2005 National Teacher of the Year

I believe that teachers should avoid the "I am master" approach and work to facilitate growth by posing critical questions, tolerating ambiguity, exploring real-world situations, encouraging student decision-making in assignments and assessments, and always being open to alternative ways of thinking.

—Brittany E. Ray, 2007 Maine Teacher of the Year

The key to everything is patience. You get the chicken by hatching the egg—not by smashing it.

—Ellen Glasgow, author

When angry, count ten, before you speak;
if very angry, an hundred.

—*President Thomas Jefferson*

The shell must be cracked apart if what is in it is to come out, for if you want the kernel you must break the shell.

—MEISTER ECKHART (ECKHART VON HOCHHEIM), THEOLOGIAN

The benefits gained from learning how to manage conflict constructively far outweigh the costs of learning time lost by students being upset and angry.

—Thomas J. Sergiovanni, educator

Do not train a child to learn by force or harshness; but direct them to it by what amuses their minds, so that you may be better able to discover with accuracy the peculiar bent of the genius of each.

—Plato, philosopher

When I taught in a public high school for three years I always ate lunch with a different group of students whether they were in my class or not, until I got to know most of them. The teachers thought I was idiotic, but they didn't realize that it actually made it easier for me to teach, that before I could effectively discipline students, I had to earn their friendship and respect.

—Marva Collins, educator

Love them enough to risk their not liking you. Children must know that there are consequences to be suffered when they are not nice.

—Carol Avila, 1995 Presidential Award winner for Excellence in Science Teaching

Let the no! once pronounced, be as a brazen wall, against which when a child hath some few times exhausted his strength without making any impression, he will never attempt to overthrow it again.

—Jean Jacques Rousseau, philosopher

I learned that it is the weak who are cruel, and that gentleness is to be expected only from the strong.

—Leo Rosten, writer

Advice and Accountability

Sometimes parents require new teachers to earn their trust.
They view us as experimenting with their kid. If you show
them you really care, then they are supportive.

—MIKE BENEVENTO, EDUCATOR

Don't plan to change the world in your first year of teaching;
it can be crushing when you find out it isn't going to happen.

—*Paul F. Cain, 2008 Texas Teacher of the Year*

**Our profession is one of the few that eats its young.
We often fail to properly prepare and support new
teachers. Good teachers are uniquely individual and
we must nurture and support each new teacher as that
person develops.**

—Michele Forman, 2001 National Teacher of the Year

Seek help. Always question us veteran teachers and we will find the answers together.

—Carol Avila, 1995 Presidential Award winner for Excellence in Science Teaching

Knock on the door of the teachers around you. Don't be a hermit and don't take it all on yourself.

—Eric A. Combs, 2007 Ohio Teacher of the Year

Allow yourself to be taught.

—Greg Evans, writer

My first year has been as disappointing as it was rewarding . . . I have lost and found hope, reviewed and revised, and finally concluded that my presence here is much more important than I had thought it would be.

—CATHERINE MCTAMANEY, EDUCATOR

First-year teachers typically experience an emotional roller coaster that begins in anxious anticipation, and cycles through survival, disillusionment, and, with luck and adequate support, rejuvenation and reflection.

—GARY BLOOM AND BARBARA DAVIS, EDUCATORS

I have been maturing as a teacher.
New experiences bring new sensitivities and flexibility . . .

—*Howard Lester, first-year teacher*

Positive feedback will keep teachers motivated and encourage more teachers to share their success with teachers who might need it and benefit from their success.

—Thomas R. Smigiel Jr., 2008 Virginia Teacher of the Year

Experienced teachers . . . are an invaluable resource to the [first-year] teachers who are willing to admit that they have much to learn.

—Robert Gress, educator

Teachers committed to excellence recognize the importance of reflection. Reflecting on students, classes, materials, successes, failures, and more ensures that we continue to grow.

—Brittany E. Ray, 2007 Maine Teacher of the Year

There are some qualities which every teacher ought to possess—or train himself to possess. These are the qualities which he wants his pupils to acquire. The young learn much by the silent power of example.

—Gilbert Highet, writer

Being a great teacher means that you share your knowledge with others and learn from as many experiences as you can so that you can continue to be a lifelong learner yourself.

—Pascale Creek Pinner, 2008 Hawaii Teacher of the Year

He that is taught only by himself has a fool for a master.

—Ben Jonson, poet

Being a teacher requires an honest soul-searching of yourself. Are you ready to go into teaching? And after you have been a teacher you have to do some soul-searching every now and then.

—Mitsuye Conover, 2000 Oklahoma Teacher of the Year

Fatigue is the price of leadership. Mediocrity is the price of never getting tired.

—John Oswald Sanders, missionary and author

Don't get too comfortable with the status quo; things could, and will, change tomorrow.

—*Charlotte Mohling, 2007 South Dakota Teacher of the Year*

In reality, our schools are just empty, impersonal places. It is the students, the teachers, and the principals who bring them to life and give them an identity.

—Philip Bigler, 1998 National Teacher of the Year

Teachers long for respect and the autonomy that comes from it. They want the limits of their professional domain clearly outlined and their essential authority within it assured. They want physical, psychological, and economic protection.

—Ted Sizer, educator

You teach best what you need to learn.
—Richard Bach, writer

Just as Plato instructed Aristotle, who taught countless others, as educators, the cycle of repeated learning and imparted wisdom is our burden and our joy to continue.

—Sharon M. Draper, 1997 National Teacher of the Year

Access your allies—get to know people who can help you on your journey to success.

—Charlotte Mohling, 2007 South Dakota Teacher of the Year

If our education system is to encourage the critical thinking necessary for a dynamic democracy, if we are to help all students reach their highest human potential, if we are to envision education as the means of transforming lives, now more than ever, we must draw the best minds and hearts into teaching and make education competitive with other professions.

—Vicki Lynn Goldsmith, 2005 Iowa Teacher of the Year

While teachers struggle to learn new methods and approaches, there is less time for students.

—David Elkind, child psychologist

Sometimes you have to fly under the radar, close your door, teach how you want to teach, but don't make too much noise about what you're doing. Then, once your kids have high test scores, then you're going to have respect, then your principal will trust you and trust what you're doing.

—Ron Clark, 2001 Disney National Teacher of the Year

I have taught 20,000 classes; I have been "evaluated" thirty times; but I have never seen another teacher teach.

—Linda Darling Hammond, educator

Outstanding teachers maintain enthusiasm
even in the face of adversity.

—*Brittany E. Ray, 2007 Maine Teacher of the Year*

A good teacher is a good student first. By repeating his lessons, he acquires excellence.

—M. K. Soni, corporate executive and author

Become a risk-taker. Go out on a limb. Often the limb you step out on will act as a catapult and take you and your students to wonderful places you never imagined existed.

—Keil E. Hileman, 2004 Kansas Teacher of the Year

There are two sides to every story
and TRUTH lays somewhere in the middle.

—*Jean Gati*

Within every school there is a sleeping giant of teacher leadership, which can be a strong catalyst for making change.

—Marilyn Katzenmeyer, educator

A new paradigm in which teacher leadership is at the vanguard of developing highly competent teachers is needed.

—Anthony Mullen, 2009 National Teacher of the Year

People's behavior makes sense if you think about it in terms of their goals, needs, and motives.

—Thomas Mann, author

If you push at the wrong time, it will backfire.

—Seth Berg, 2008 Colorado Teacher of the Year

If a doctor, lawyer, or dentist had 40 people in his office at one time, all of whom had different needs, and some of whom didn't want to be there and were causing trouble, and the doctor, lawyer, or dentist, without assistance, had to treat them all with professional excellence for nine months, then he might have some conception of the classroom teacher's job.

—Donald D. Quinn, educator

However much the teacher is tempted to treat the exceptional pupil (whether very good or very bad) as a special case and to devote to him or her a great deal of time and attention, he must remember that this is not his sole duty, and usually is not his main duty. His first obligation is to his class: to the group.

—Gilbert Highet, writer

Be not angry that you cannot make others as you wish them to be, since you cannot make yourself as you wish to be.

—Thomas A. Kempis, theologian

Few things help an individual more than to place responsibility upon him, and to let him know that you trust him.

—*Booker T. Washington, educator*

Good teaching must be slow enough so that it is not confusing, and fast enough so that it is not boring.

—Sidney J. Harris, journalist

I'm a tough teacher, but if I want them to be nice to each other, I better be the nicest guy they ever met.

—Rafe Esquith, 1992 Disney National Teacher of the Year

If I compliment them, I mean it. If I don't think they are doing a good job, I lay it on the line. I demand respect from them and I give them respect, and I think they are important.

—LENNI ABEL, 2000 DISNEY NATIONAL TEACHER OF THE YEAR

I let the kids know exactly what I expect.
I praise them when they meet those expectations and point it out to them when they don't.

—Ron Clark, 2001 Disney National Teacher of the Year

You can preach at them: that is a hook without a worm; you can order them to volunteer: that is dishonest; you can call upon them: you are needed, and that approach will hardly ever fail.

—Kurt Hahn, educator

I have one rule—attention. They give me theirs and I give them mine.

—Sister Evangelist, educator

Teachers who act as if they have something to learn as well as something to contribute, establish better learning relationships with students and parents.

—Andy Hargreaves and Michael Fullan, educators

The kids are proud of the trust I give them, and they do not want to lose it. They rarely do, and I make sure on a daily basis that I deserve the trust I ask of them.

—RAFE ESQUITH, 1992 DISNEY NATIONAL TEACHER OF THE YEAR

Many instructional arrangements seem "contrived," but there is nothing wrong with that. It is the teacher's function to contrive conditions under which students learn. It has always been the task of formal education to set up behavior which would prove useful or enjoyable later in a student's life.

—B.F. Skinner, psychologist

No use to shout at them to pay attention. If the situations, the materials, the problems before the child do not interest him, his attention will slip off to what does interest him, and no amount of exhortation of threats will bring it back.

—John Holt, educator

Teachers must also hold themselves as accountable for high-quality teaching as they hold students for high-quality learning performances.

—Melanie Teemant, 2007 Nevada Teacher of the Year

The first key in solving any training problem is to diagnose it correctly.

—Stephen R. Covey, writer

Human beings are full of emotion, and the teacher who knows how to use it will have dedicated learners. It means sending dominant signals instead of submissive ones with your eyes, body and voice.

—Leon Lessinger, writer

Education is the point at which we decide whether we love the world enough to assume responsibility for it.
—Hannah Arendt, political scientist

In communities the best discipline strategies are those that teach students citizenship and help students become caring adults. Key are the standards, values, and commitments that make up a constitution for living together

—THOMAS J. SERGIOVANNI, EDUCATOR

No one sets higher standards for students or higher accountability for teachers than effective teachers do—for it is teachers who suffer the most from a lack of accountability.

—Andy Baumgartner, 1999 National Teacher of the Year

Teachers are expected to reach unattainable goals with inadequate tools. The miracle is that at times they accomplish this impossible task.

—Haim G. Ginott, child psychologist

What is needed, then, is a model of accountability that gives teachers the room they need to develop a personalized pedagogy . . . while simultaneously requiring clear evidence of academic growth for every child.

—Joshua M. Anderson, 2007 Kansas Teacher of the Year

Teenagers go to college to be with their boyfriends and girlfriends; they go because they can't think of anything else to do; they go because their parents want them to and sometimes because their parents don't want them to; they go to find themselves, or to find a husband, or to get away from home, and sometimes even to find out about the world in which they live.

—Harold Howe II, U.S. Commissioner of Education

I possess the power to lace their intake with arsenic or sweet nectar, creating their self-esteem or destroying it. I shudder under the burden of such a responsibility.

—Rae Ellen McKee, 1991 National Teacher of the Year

I never release control of my class to the students by blaming them for being "lazy and unmotivated" or that they "need to be held accountable"—nor do I allow them to use excuses, either. The work we do is too important.

—Tamara Steen, 2005 Washington Teacher of the Year

Our children are spending way too much time unaccompanied or in solitude.

—Ina B. Bouker, 2007 Alaska Teacher of the Year

Let parents then bequeath to their children not riches, but the spirit of reverence.

—Plato, philosopher

I must be held accountable for making certain that the children in my classroom experience every opportunity to learn to trust educators and to develop a joy of learning!

—Andy Baumgartner, 1999 National Teacher of the Year

We will never truly know how many students' lives
are changed by our sense of responsibility.

—*Marilyn Jachetti Whirry, 2000 National Teacher of the Year*

**He wanted everyone to know that he was at the school
and of it, and that because of him and through the sheer
force of his personality, the school was going to get better,
improve, blaze into the heavens . . .**

—Thom Jones, writer

A child educated only at school is an uneducated child.
—George Santayana, philosopher

Contrast to doctors and lawyers that work in the public eye—
teachers can lose sponges or amputate the wrong limb with no
witnesses except the victim.

—Parker Palmer, educator

I have helped to prevent many inappropriate special education referrals, by questioning teachers to find the roots of their students' problems and providing suggestions for intervening and adapting lessons to match the students' needs.

—Tamra A. Tiong, 2007 New Mexico Teacher of the Year

Teachers who fail to improve, whether from poor preparation, burnout, or lack of professionalism and who are judged to be ineffective must be counseled out of the profession in order to ensure students' success in school.

—Thomas R. Smigiel Jr., 2008 Virginia Teacher of the Year

Whether you are a middle-class suburbanite, a parent living in the slums of a major city or a resident of a rural area, your involvement will mean that your child will learn more and do better in school.

—Melitta J. Cutright, writer

An ineffective teacher on the grade level below is a poor base on which to build. An ineffective teacher on the grade level above is work and time gone to waste.

—Andy Baumgartner, 1999 National Teacher of the Year

The real measure of a teacher is not that the kids like him or that they do well at the tests at the end of the year. The real measure is where are these children five years from now, ten years from now?

—Rafe Esquith, 1992 Disney National Teacher of the Year

Students have as much responsibility
as the educators in their schools.

—*Lee J. James, 2006 Mississippi Teacher of the Year*

No matter how good teaching may be, each student must take the responsibility for his own education.

—John Carolus S. J.

Education commences at the mother's knee, and every word spoken within the hearing of little children tends towards the formation of character.

—Hosea Ballou, theologian

The success of our schools depends on our essential partnership with families and the community.

—Kathy Mellor, 2004 National Teacher of the Year

Schools are to prepare the young for the future, for earthly conditions as they will be, not as they were, for manhood appropriate to a future rather than to a present time, for values relevant to the inevitably changing conditions that will obtain two or four or more decades hence.

—Ted Sizer, educator

Education is a progressive discovery of our own ignorance.

—Will Durant, philosopher

I tell the parents, "that kid belongs to you. He doesn't belong to the state or the school, he's your kid. So you have to help me out to raise this kid. To ask him what he has to do."

—Jaime Escalante, educator

Many theorists have written about education as if it were chiefly intended to teach young people to live in society. Yet it is clear, when we look at young men and women, that they also need to be taught how to live with themselves.

—Gilbert Highet, writer

In West Germany . . . only 9 percent of the age cohort reached their terminal year of high school in the early 1970s, whereas in the U.S. approximately 75 percent did. It should not be surprising that a more academically select group would perform better than the average U.S. student.

—Chester E. Finn Jr., educator

We are in danger of becoming a national institution
purely devoted to producing empty children
with outstanding test scores.

—*Joshua M. Anderson, 2007 Kansas Teacher of the Year*

*Nobody is paying attention to the individual adolescent,
but everyone is hysterical about the aggregate.*

— Patricia Hersch, writer

A natural temptation is to look for a scapegoat when things are not
going well. . . . parents blame teachers. . . . teachers blame parents. . . .
but placing blame on any group is not going to get us anywhere.

—David Walsh, psychologist

I expect quality work, just as an employer would.

—Charlotte Mohling, 2007 South Dakota Teacher of the Year

Compassionate teachers fill a void left by working parents who aren't able to devote enough attention to their children. A good education consists of much more than useful facts and marketable skills.

—Charles Platt, author

Failure to educate all students is everyone's failure. We must share in the responsibility or share the repercussions.

—Kathy Mellor, 2004 National Teacher of the Year

I was always prepared for success but that means that I have to be prepared for failure, too.

—*Shel Silverstein, author and illustrator*

When snapshot-style testing can determine whether or not a student is eligible to graduate from high school, we are leaving students behind.

—Brittany E. Ray, 2007 Maine Teacher of the Year

Where there is an open mind there will ⌐

—Charles F. Kettering, educa

I believe that the testing of the student's
in order to see if he meets some criterioi
teacher, is directly contrary to the implications of therapy
for significant learning.

—Carl Rogers, psychologist

We think too much about effective methods of teaching and
not enough about effective methods of learning.

—John Carolus S.J.

By providing a safe environment, rich with activities and infused
with mutual respect and acceptance, then, and only then, will no
child be left behind.

—Karen Ginty, 2007 New Jersey Teacher of the Year

...ntary school must assume as its sublime and ...lemn responsibility the task of teaching every ...d in it to read. Any school that does not accomplish this has failed.

—William J. Bennett, political scientist

A university's essential character is that of being a center of free inquiry and criticism—a thing not to be sacrificed for anything else.

—RICHARD HOFSTADTER, HISTORIAN

Learning as a Process

I believe that the future of our nation depends upon our citizens' ability to think, rather than repeat learned information. Thus, education must motivate students to love the learning process.

—Rae Ellen McKee, 1991 National Teacher of the Year

He then learns that in going down into the secrets of his own mind he has descended into the secrets of all minds.

—Ralph Waldo Emerson, philosopher

Learning is not attained by chance, it must be sought for with ardor and attended to with diligence.

—First Lady Abigail Adams

Your best teacher is your last mistake.

—Ralph Nader, social activist

The only person who is educated is the one who has learned how to learn and change.

—**Carl Rogers, psychologist**

Towering genius disdains a beaten path. It seeks regions hitherto unexplored.

—President Abraham Lincoln

No great genius has ever existed without some touch of madness.

—*Aristotle, philosopher*

Information is without value until a community of learners receives it, reflects on it, and makes it a part of their lives. Then, and only then, does it become knowledge.

—Thomas A. Fleming, 1992 National Teacher of the Year

True genius resides in the capacity for evaluation of uncertain, hazardous, and conflicting information.

—Prime Minister Winston Churchill

Passion is the genesis of genius.

—Tony Robbins, writer

It must be remembered that the purpose of education is not to fill the minds of students with facts . . . it is to teach them to think, if that is possible, and always to think for themselves.

—Robert Hutchins, educator

Knowledge comes, but wisdom lingers.

—Alfred Tennyson, poet

The beginning is the most important part of the work.

Plato, philosopher

Even without success, creative persons find joy in a job well done. Learning for its own sake is rewarding.

—Mihaly Csikszentmihalyi, psychologist

The wisest mind has something yet to learn.

—George Santayana, philosopher

Learning is often spoken of as if we were watching the open pages of all the books which we have ever read, and then, when occasion arises, we select the right page to read aloud to the universe.

—Alfred North Whitehead, philosopher and mathematician

Learning occurs at the moment of wonder.

—George Edwin Goodfellow, 2008 Rhode Island Teacher of the Year

Learning by discovery can occur without help,
but only geniuses can educate themselves without
the help of teachers.

—*Mortimer J. Adler, educator*

They know enough who know how to learn.
—*Henry Adams, writer*

**For many, learning is a spiral, where important themes
are visited again and again throughout life, each time at a
deeper, more penetrating level.**

—Jerold W. Aps, educator

I cannot teach anybody anything, I can only make them think.

—SOCRATES, PHILOSOPHER

It is by extending oneself, by exercising some capacity previously unused that you come to a better knowledge of your own potential.

—Harold Bloom, literary theorist

Learning without thought is labor lost.

—*Confucius, philosopher*

Art is not to be taught in Academies. It is what one looks at, not what one listens to, that makes the artist. The real schools should be the streets.

—Oscar Wilde, playwright

If we succeed in giving the love of learning, the learning itself is sure to follow.

—John Lubbock, politician

A man should never be ashamed to own he has been wrong, which is but saying in other words that he is wiser today than he was yesterday.

—Alexander Pope, poet

To think is to differ.

—Clarence Darrow, defense attorney

Teachers must be able to inspire their students to excellence, showing them a world that is bigger than their own.

—ANDREA PETERSON, 2007 WASHINGTON TEACHER OF THE YEAR

The origin of thinking is some perplexity, confusion or doubt.

—John Dewey, educational philosopher

I am not ashamed to confess that I am
ignorant of what I do not know.

—*Marcus T. Cicero, philosopher*

**It is much simpler to buy books than to read them and
easier to read them than to absorb their contents. Too
many men slip early out of the habit of studious reading,
and yet that is essential . . .**

—William Osler, physician

It's what you learn after you know it all that counts.

—President Harry S Truman

Wonder is the desire for knowledge.
                    —St. Thomas Aquinas, theologian

Read not to contradict and confute, nor to believe and take for granted . . . but to weigh and consider.
                    —FRANCIS BACON, PHILOSOPHER

Learning is never done without errors and defeat.
                    —Vladimir Lenin, politician

The mind grows by what it feeds on.
                    —J.G. Holland, writer

Never discourage anyone who continually makes progress, no matter how slow.
                    —Plato, philosopher

Do not confuse excellence with perfection; remind your students that failure is just another opportunity to try again.

—Lois J. Rebich, 2007 Pennsylvania Teacher of the Year

Students need to learn to experience solitude and to sit in discomfort to examine the source of an idea.

—Vicki Lynn Goldsmith, 2005 Iowa Teacher of the Year

The educator must above all understand how to wait; to reckon all effects in the light of the future, not of the present.

—ELLEN KEY, WRITER

I was taught that the way of progress is neither swift nor easy.

—*Marie Curie, scientist*

Only the curious will learn and only the resolute over-come the obstacles to learning. The quest quotient has always excited me more than the intelligence quotient.
—Eugene S. Wilson, educator, as quoted in the *Reader's Digest* (1968)

One can think effectively only when one is willing to endure suspense and to undergo the trouble of searching.
—JOHN DEWEY, EDUCATIONAL PHILOSOPHER

Often times, the learning happens in these uncomfortable moments. That's what the silence is for.
—Mallory Buckingham, speech pathologist

Too often, for too many of us, learning appears to be an imposition, a surrender of our own will power to external direction, indeed a sort of enslavement.
—Gilbert Highet, writer

The shrewd guess, the fertile hypothesis, the courageous leap to a tentative conclusion—these are the most valuable coins of the thinker at work. But in most schools guessing is heavily penalized and is associated somehow with laziness.

—Jerome Bruner, psychologist

The beloved and remembered teacher instills in students an unquenchable thirst for learning and a resilient desire for success.

—Andy Baumgartner, 1999 National Teacher of the Year

One must learn by doing the thing, for though you think you know it, you have no certainty until you try.

—*Aristotle, philosopher*

In all things we learn only from those we love.
—Johann Wolfgang von Goethe, philosopher

A teacher must project passion in the classroom because this powerful emotion sparks the learning process in children and motivates them to remember key concepts and ideas.

—Anthony J. Mullen, 2009 National Teacher of the Year

Anxiety checks learning. An overall feeling of inferiority, a temporary humiliation, a fit of depression, defiance or anger, a sense of being rejected, and many other emotional disturbances affect the learning process. The reverse is true; a feeling of well-being and of being respected by others stimulates an alert mind, willingness to participate, and an attitude conducive to learning.

—EDA LESHAN, WRITER

My advice to kids who want to become authors and to kids who just want to write well just for fun is to read. I think that we really learn how to write by reading.

—Joanna Cole, children's author

Reading well makes children more interesting both to themselves and others, a process in which they will develop a sense of being separate and distinct selves.

—Harold Bloom, literary theorist

We learn to do something by doing it. There is no other way.

—*John Holt, educator*

True interest appears when the self identifies itself with ideas or objects, when it finds in them a means of expression and they become a necessary form of fuel for its activity.

—JEAN PIAGET, CHILD PSYCHOLOGIST

Most of the most important experiences that truly educate cannot be arranged ahead of time with any precision.

—*Harold Taylor, educator and social activist*

The very fact of its [the human mind's] finding itself in agreement with other minds perturbs it, so that it hunts for points of divergence, feeling the urgent need to make it clear that at least it reached the same conclusions by a different route.

—**Herbert Butterfield, historian**

Learning proceeds in fits and starts.

—*Jerold W. Aps, educator*

We learn simply by the exposure of living, and what we learn most natively is the tradition in which we live.

—*David P. Gardner, educator*

Modeling is the way every child learns, from how to tie a shoe to how to drive a car.

—Steve Gardiner, 2008 Montana Teacher of the Year

Learning is like rowing upstream. Advance or lose all.
—Anonymous

Learning is always rebellion . . .
Every bit of new truth discovered is
revolutionary to what was believed before.

—*Margaret Lee Runbeck, writer*

If we want graduates to think of art, literature, and history
as ways to solve problems, we must examine what is worth
knowing, doing, and becoming.

—Vicki Lynn Goldsmith, 2005 Iowa Teacher of the Year

**By the age of ten the brain may actually start to destroy
unused synapses.**

Dr. Jerry Graniero, educator

By learning you will teach, by teaching you will learn.

—Latin proverb

When asked what learning was the most necessary, he said, "Not to unlearn what you have learned!"

—Diogenes Laertius, biographer

The biggest kick in teaching comes when I look into the face of a young child and watch confusion turn to concentration, concentration to surprise, and finally surprise into the pride of accomplishment.

—Andy Baumgartner, 1999 National Teacher of the Year

Reading without reflecting is like eating without digesting.

—Edmund Burke, political scientist

Education . . . is a painful, continual and difficult work to be done in kindness, by watching, by warning, . . . by praise, but above all, by example.

—John Ruskin, art critic and social theorist

No one can become really educated without having pursued some study in which he took no interest.

—T.S. Eliot, poet

You know a teacher is doing a reasonable job when he finds his students can get along fine without him.

—J. J. Dewey, writer

Give me four years to teach the children
and the seed I have sown will never be uprooted.

—*Vladimir Lenin, politician*

In the practical use of our intellect, forgetting is as important as remembering.

—William James, psychologist

"Intent" is a lesson in itself. "Intentions" are not sustainable unless the act is complete!

—Carl Stoynoff, poet

All practical teachers know that education is a patient process of mastery of details, minute by minute, hour by hour, day by day.

—Alfred North Whitehead, philosopher and mathematician

Teaching is complex and dynamic, demanding constant reflection and adjustment. My students and I work collaboratively toward the common goal of learning.

—MICHELE FORMAN, 2001 NATIONAL TEACHER OF THE YEAR

Learning is a social process that occurs through interpersonal interaction within a cooperative context. Individuals, working together, construct shared understandings and knowledge.

—David Johnson, educational psychologist

I believe that children learn best when given the opportunity to taste, feel, see, hear, manipulate, discover, sing, and dance their way through learning.

—Katy Goldman, educator

I have always believed that in order to really understand a concept, a person should hear it, see it, and do it, and that is what I try to do with the concepts I teach.

—Eric Kincaid, 2008 West Virginia Teacher of the Year

I don't teach to the test. I teach my kids content. And I make it as fun and exciting as I can.

—Ron Clark, 2001 Disney National Teacher of the Year

It's not that I'm so smart, it's just that I stay with problems longer.

—Albert Einstein, physicist

The essence of learning is the ability to manage change by changing yourself.

—ARIE DE GUES, CORPORATE EXECUTIVE

He is educated who knows where to find out
what he doesn't know.

—Georg Simmel, sociologist

How sustained an episode a learner is willing to undergo depends upon what the person expects to get from his efforts, in the sense of such external things as grades but also in the sense of a gain in understanding.

—Jerome S. Bruner, psychologist

The illiterate of the 21st century will not be those who cannot read and write, but those who cannot learn, unlearn, and relearn.

—Alvin Toffler, writer

Where I grew up, learning was a collective activity. But when I got to school and tried to share learning with other students that was called cheating. The curriculum sent the clear message to me that learning was a highly individualistic, almost secretive, endeavor.

—Henry A. Giroux, educator

Try to put into practice what you already know,
and in so doing you will in good time discover
the hidden things which you now inquire about.

—Henry Van Dyke, writer

Mistakes are the portals of discovery.

—James Joyce, author

If a man will begin with certainties, he shall end in doubts; but if he will be content to begin with doubts, he shall end in certainties.

—Francis Bacon, philosopher

To every answer you can find a new question.

—*Yiddish proverb*

Every student has a right to find some element of success in his or her school career, since this is most often the major prerequisite to finding success in life.

—Andy Baumgartner, 1999 National Teacher of the Year

Our errors are surely not such awfully solemn things. In a world where we are so certain to incur them in spite of all our caution, a certain lightness of heart seems healthier than this excessive nervousness on their behalf.

—William James, psychologist

I have learned throughout my life as a composer chiefly through my mistakes and pursuits of false assumptions, not my exposure to founts of wisdom and knowledge.

—Igor Stravinsky, composer

Every act of conscious learning requires the willingness to suffer an injury to one's self-esteem. That is why young children, before they are aware of their own self-importance learn so easily; and why older persons, especially if vain or important, cannot learn at all.

—THOMAS SZASZ, PSYCHOLOGIST

It is what we think we know already that often prevents us from learning.

—Claude Bernard, physiologist

The result of the educative process is capacity for further education.

—John Dewey, educational philosopher

I find that a great part of the information I have was acquired by looking up something and finding something else on the way.

—Franklin Pierce Adams, journalist

I believe that students should have 'LOTS' (lower order thinking skills) before they can have 'HOTS' (higher order thinking skills) and that education should be a hands-on process where students learn by experiencing.

—Mark A. Nethercott, 2007 Wyoming Teacher of the Year

I am still learning.

—*Michelangelo di Lodovico Buonarroti Simoni, artist*

In completing one discovery we never fail to get an imperfect knowledge of others of which we could have no idea before, so that we cannot solve one doubt without creating several new ones.

—Joseph Priestly, theologian

In its broadest sense, learning can be defined as a process of progressive change from ignorance to knowledge, from inability to competence, and from indifference to understanding.

—Cameron Fincher, educator

Education is a lifelong process of which schooling is only a small but necessary part. As long as one remains alive and healthy, learning can go on—and should.

—Mortimer J. Adler, educator

Education is man's going forward from cocksure ignorance to thoughtful uncertainty.

—*Kenneth G. Johnson, communication theorist*

That is the essence of science: ask an impertinent question, and you are on the way to a pertinent answer.

—Jacob Bronowski, scientist and mathematician

That's what learning is, after all; not whether we lose the game, but how we lose and how we've changed because of it and what we take away from it that we never had before . . .

—RICHARD BACH, WRITER

Much that passes for education . . . is not education at all but ritual. The fact is that we are being educated when we know it least.

—David P. Gardner, educator

Doing It for the Kids

I often praise the children by telling them
my heart is singing.

—*Karen Ginty, 2007 New Jersey Teacher of the Year*

**I determined that there should not be a minute in the day
when my children should not be aware of my face and my
lips that my heart was theirs, that their happiness was my
happiness, and their pleasures my pleasures.**

—Johann Heinrich Pestalozzi, educator

Choose to celebrate the strengths in those around you.

—Ann Marie H. Taylor, 2008 South Carolina Teacher of the Year

Teacher: The child's third parent.

—*Hyman Berston, professor of real estate*

Working with a teacher is often a student's first professional relationship, and a successful one gives them the courage to form additional ones.

—Carolyn Kelley, 2007 New Hampshire Teacher of the Year

Morality sticks faster when presented in brief sayings than when presented in long discourse.

— Karl Leberecht Immermann, author

Endeavor, first, to broaden your children's sympathies and, by satisfying their daily needs, to bring love and kindness into such unceasing contact with their impressions and their activity, that these sentiments may be engrafted in their hearts.

—Johann Heinrich Pestalozzi, educator

You can lead a horse to water but you can't make him drink. It's our job as teachers to at least make him thirsty.

—Seth Berg, 2008 Colorado Teacher of the Year

No one has yet realized the wealth of sympathy, the kindness and generosity hidden in the soul of a child. The effort of every true education should be to unlock that treasure.

—Emma Goldman, anarchist

If I am right about everything, and you believe it and follow the teachings without confirmation from within, you have found nothing.

—J. J. Dewey, writer

When you introduce a moral lesson, let it be brief.

—Horace, poet

I hated high school. I didn't have any friends because I didn't fit in, but I enjoyed the educational part of it. My teachers allowed me to be creative, so I thought past high school to what I wanted to do.

—CHAD MICHAEL MURRAY, ACTOR

Adolescence is a sloppy time. A kid can easily be part child and part adult. Two kids the same age can be years apart.

—Patricia Hersch, writer

Students who are engaged and invested in what they're doing find their own voices.

—*Vicki Lynn Goldsmith, 2005 Iowa Teacher of the Year*

When students are interested, they start to ask real questions. And when they ask questions, they're on their way to becoming great scientists and learners.

—Michael Geisen, 2008 National Teacher of the Year

Once kids get excited and curious about learning, everything else will more or less fall into place, even motivation and grades.

—Michael Riera, educator

I hold the values of our culture and the history of our world before them like a sweet confection.

—Rae Ellen McKee, 1991 National Teacher of the Year

I am a firm believer that nearly every student will rise to the level of expectations placed on her or him, and my students continue to confirm this at every opportunity.

—Tracey Leon Bailey, 1993 National Teacher of the Year

There are kids all over this country who have never been told that they have potential. Many of them will grow up to settle for a job, not a career, because no one has taught them to value themselves or helped them see what they can do.

—Sandra L. McBrayer, 1994 National Teacher of the Year

My philosophy is just don't give up. I just don't give up on anybody. Failure's not an option.

—Mary Schlieder, 2008 Nebraska Teacher of the Year

To open the minds and spirits of our young people, we must help them feel love for the search for knowledge—a search to know the what and the why, to understand the hearts and minds of others, and to understand the meaning of the world and our place in it.

—Marilyn Jachetti Whirry, 2000 National Teacher of the Year

The students in my class know that can't is not an option . . . I teach them that if there is a wall in their way, they can go around it, over it, under it, or through it, but they can never be stopped by it.

—Melanie Teemant, 2007 Nevada Teacher of the Year

Young people need much more to be demanded of them. They need to be needed, they need to give, they need opportunities to show love, courage, sacrifice. They need to be part of a cause that is larger than the sum of their individual appetites. They need to believe in something.

—THOMAS SOBOL, EDUCATOR

Once you prove to them that they are not inferior, just different they can soar in ways you never expected.

—George Edwin Goodfellow, 2008 Rhode Island Teacher of the Year

Children are like wet cement, whatever falls on them makes an impression.

—*Haim Ginott, child psychologist*

I love to feel proud: proud of a child who learns the English language, proud of a child who makes the perfect M, proud of a child who acts like a friend and can be a model for the class, proud of a child who learns his or her line for the school play.

—KAREN GUARDINO, KINDERGARTEN TEACHER

Every child's life is like a piece of paper on which every person leaves a mark.

—Chinese proverb

I tell my students that our class is like a wagon train heading out across this great expanse of learning to reach our goal: an education. No one will be thrown overboard; no one will be left behind. Together we are all going to get there.

—Chauncey Veatch, 2002 National Teacher of the Year

The effective teacher always considers the needs of his or her students first!

—Andy Baumgartner, 1999 National Teacher of the Year

I expect a level of effort, critical thinking, and academic excellence from every child in my class that might seem more appropriate to a Gifted and Talented program or elite private school.

—Justin Minkel, 2007 Arkansas Teacher of the Year

Think well and do good.

JOHN DELAP, PRINCIPAL AT FAYETTEVILLE HIGH SCHOOL

When a student knows that you set high standards, and when they know you care about them, I have found them to be magnificent achievers.

—Eric A. Combs, 2007 Ohio Teacher of the Year

Set clear (and high!) expectations for your students . . . Once you set the bar high, children inevitably rise to the occasion.

—Jason Kamras, 2005 National Teacher of the Year

Our students need training in resistance skills. Those include being able to defy negative peer pressure and dangerous community influences.

—Ina B. Bouker, 2007 Alaska Teacher of the Year

Children's talent to endure stems from their ignorance of alternatives.

—Maya Angelou, poet

None of my other teachers held me up to the same standard as my English teacher, Ms. Tsang. I eventually learned to hold myself up to the same standard.

—Melissa Macomber, social worker

I don't think we expect enough of students. There are a lot of fabulous young people out there. They just need someone to show them the way.

—Rafe Esquith, 1992 Disney National Teacher of the Year

I can still hear the elders saying to us
that we must learn how to make decisions!

—Ina B. Bouker, 2007 Alaska Teacher of the Year

I must make every effort to challenge the stronger students to strive toward further progress and to patiently love the struggling students into persevering.

—Andy Baumgartner, 1999 National Teacher of the Year

Murray Cohn has, for twenty-three years, run Brandeis according to his own lights. . . . He believes in publicly praising achievement—and the school's bulletin boards offer congratulations to attendance leaders and the like. What Cohn and other administrators like him impart to their schools is nothing quantifiable; it is an ethos.

—James Traub, journalist

The potential possibilities of any child are the most intriguing and stimulating in all creation.
—Ray L. Wilbur, physician

Children are liquid. They shape themselves to fit the form of the container into which they are placed . . . I am forever indebted to my teachers. They had enough faith to swing the bucket, because they knew that it was in the very nature of the water to remain right there.

—Paula Polk Lillard, educator

Kids today are oriented to immediacy. Theirs is a world of fast foods, fast music, fast cars, fast relationships and fast gratification. They are not buying our promise for tomorrow because they don't think we can deliver . . .

—LeRoy E. Hay, 1983 National Teacher of the Year

There is always one moment in childhood when the door opens and lets the future in.

—*Graham Greene, author*

Children and adults alike share needs to be safe and secure; to belong and to be loved; to experience self-esteem through achievement, mastery, recognition, and respect; to be autonomous; and to experience self-actualization by pursuing one's inner abilities and finding intrinsic meaning and satisfaction in what one does.

—Thomas J. Sergiovanni, educator

The intellectual development of the child is no clockwork sequence of events; it also responds to influences from the environment, notably the school environment.

—Jerome S. Bruner, psychologist

I am old-fashioned and romantic enough to believe that many children, given the right circumstances, are natural readers until this instinct is destroyed by the media. It may be an illusion to believe that the magical connection of solitary children to the best books can endure, but such a relationship does go so long a way back that it will not easily expire.

—Harold Bloom, literary theorist

I want my kids to work hard, so I've got to be the hardest worker they've ever seen.

—Rafe Esquith,
1992 Disney National Teacher of the Year

Reading, in contrast to sitting before the screen, is not a purely passive exercise. The child, particularly one who reads a book dealing with real life, has nothing before it but the hieroglyphics of the printed page. Imagination must do the rest; and imagination is called upon to do it.

—GEORGE F. KENNAN, POLITICAL SCIENTIST

We save a boy's soul at the same time we are saving his algebra.

—George C. St. John, educator

If it be urged that some men have such weak intellects that it is not possible for them to acquire knowledge, I answer that it is scarcely possible to find a mirror so dulled that it will not reflect images of some kind, or for a tablet to have such a rough surface that nothing can be inscribed on it.

—John Amos Comenius, educator

I had learned to respect the intelligence, integrity, creativity and capacity for deep thought and hard work latent somewhere in every child; they had learned that I differed from them only in years and experience, and that as I, an ordinary human being, loved and respected them, I expected payment in kind.

—Sybil Marshall, educator

Your children are not your children. They are the sons and daughters of Life's longing for itself. They came through you but not from you. And though they are with you yet they belong not to you. You may give them your love but not your thoughts, for they have their own thoughts.

—Kahlil Gibran, writer

What I'm concerned about is the people who don't dwell on the meaninglessness of their lives, or the meaningfulness of it—who just pursue mindless entertainment.

—Michael K. Hooker, educator

I cannot think of any need in childhood as strong as the need for a father's protection.

—Sigmund Freud, psychologist

. . . if this world were anything near what it should be there would be no more need of a Book Week than there would be of a Society for the Prevention of Cruelty to Children.

—Dorothy Parker, writer

So long as little children are allowed to suffer, there is no true love in this world.

—Isadora Duncan, dancer

Thirty-one chances. Thirty-one futures, our futures. It's an almost psychotic feeling, believing that part of their lives belongs to me. Everything they become, I also become. And everything about me, they helped to create.

—ESMÉ RAJI CODELL, EDUCATOR

We all have duty in this world of education,
but the student alone must shoulder their own education
to whatever end they take it.

—*Eric A. Combs, 2007 Ohio Teacher of the Year*

I am humbled daily by the power of our profession. My work with my students has made me a better thinker, a daily dreamer, and a passionate believer that a good education can change a child's disposition.

—Kristin Bourguet, 2007 Arizona Teacher of the Year

The American male at the peak of his physical powers and appetites, driving 160 big white horses across the scenes of an increasingly open society, with weekend money in his pocket and with little prior exposure to trouble and tragedy, personifies "an accident going to happen."

—John Sloan Dickey, educator

The work can wait while you show the child the rainbow, but the rainbow won't wait while you do the work.

—Patricia Clafford, poet

I long remained a child,
and I am still one in many respects.

—*Jean Jacques Rousseau, philosopher*

Every teacher thinks his subject is the end-all, but ultimately I want to teach students to be good citizens involved in their community.

—Christopher Poulos, 2007 Connecticut Teacher of the Year

Never have ideas about children, and never have ideas for them.

—George Orwell, author

Such, such were the joys/When we all, girls and boys/
In our youth time were seen/On the Echoing Green.

—*William Blake, poet*

A hundred years from now it will not matter what my bank account was, the sort of house I lived in, or the kind of car I drove. . . . but the world may be different because I was important in the life of a child.

—Kathy Davis, educator

Teach a child how to think, not what to think.

—Sidney Sugarman, jurist

The job of an educator is to teach students to see the vitality in themselves.

—Joseph Campbell, mythologist

We must teach our children to dream with their eyes open.

—Harry Edwards, sociologist

A professor can never better distinguish himself in his work than by encouraging a clever pupil, for the true discoverers are among them, as comets amongst the stars.

—CARL VON LINNE (CARL LINNAEUS), SCIENTIST

We must view young people not as empty bottles to be filled, but as candles to be lit.

—*Robert H. Shaffer, educator*

The fact we must remember is that we are educating students for a world that will not be ours but will be theirs. Give them a chance to be heard.

—Carlos P. Romulo, author

They are kids!!!! That's why we call them that.

—*Laura Schlessinger, counselor and talk show host*

Why is it that with children we so quickly see the obstacles and problems and so easily miss the joys?

—Johann Christoph Arnold, writer

Small, simple, sincere gestures to all students, such as a pat on the back, a smile, a big hello, a compliment, or maybe even a few minutes to just listen without judging, can become dynamic, extraordinary acts that help constructively shape young lives. These are little things that make a big difference in the life of a child.

—Mark A. Nethercott, 2007 Wyoming Teacher of the Year

The first goal in an emergency is always to protect a child from further damage and to limit the impact of catastrophic events.

—Lauren K. Ayers, psychologist

You are rewarding a teacher poorly if you remain always a pupil.

—**Friedrich Nietzsche, philosopher**

You can catch students doing right or you can catch them doing wrong. I try to catch them doing right because we've got to build the egos of these kids so that they will want to return to school.

—Mary V. Bicouvaris, 1989 National Teacher of the Year

One kid at a time.

— Patricia Hersch, writer

Too many times young people are painfully aware of their shortcomings. These messages come from the adults in their lives and are delivered both in words and actions.

—Paul F. Cain, 2008 Texas Teacher of the Year

Remember this: no one is better than you.

—*Jaime Escalante, educator*

I believe all students should learn how to remain true to themselves in the midst of a crowd; how to hold on to their original dreams and imagination; how to share our home planet justly with all life; how to respect differences and find commonalities; how to speak with words and actions as well as with silence.

—Tamra A. Tiong, 2007 New Mexico Teacher of the Year

Let the potential artist in our children come to life that they may surmount industrial monotonies and pressures.

—Barbara Morgan, educator and astronaut

There is no such thing as a weird human being. It's just that some people require more understanding than others do.

—Tom Robbins, author

Each student is a unique person and a powerful learner capable of great achievements.

—Michele Forman, 2001 National Teacher of the Year

The most important part of our job as teachers is to introduce the community to our students and our students to the community. To do this, we must live in both worlds.

—Joshua M. Anderson, 2007 Kansas Teacher of the Year

I love to let them create meaning for themselves,
let them talk. They want to be heard.

—*Beth A. Oswald, 2008 Wisconsin Teacher of the Year*

A frequent phrase we use in the classroom is "share your kindness." If you expect children to help each other, then they will.

—Karen Ginty, 2007 New Jersey Teacher of the Year

We forget that with some natures it is necessary to train the individual, and to develop his or her special abilities: such people may never be absorbed into any group, and yet be of great service to themselves and to mankind.

—GILBERT HIGHET, WRITER

It is important that each and every student feel honored in my classroom. I create a place where students can think freely and be themselves.

—Susanne H. Frensley, 2007 Tennessee Teacher of the Year

Children, like rosebuds, bloom at different times. However, the last bloom is just as pretty as the first.

—BETSY ROGERS, 2003 NATIONAL TEACHER OF THE YEAR,
QUOTING HER FIRST-GRADE TEACHER

Child, give me your hand that I may walk in the light of your faith in me.

—Hannah Kahn, poet

Good teachers empathize with kids, respect them, and believe that each one has something special that can be built upon.

—Ann Lieberman, educator

They come to me without an inkling of what talent and power of perception they have... and very rarely has anyone ever bothered to credit their insight.

—Lenni Abel, 2000 Disney National Teacher of the Year

We worry about what a child will be tomorrow,
yet we forget that he or she is someone today.

—*Stacia Tauscher, writer*

There's honestly no group of people I'd rather get up in the morning to see every day.

—Jason Kamras, 2005 National Teacher of the Year

To be alienated is to lack a sense of belonging, to feel cut off from family, friends, school or work—the four worlds of childhood.

—Urie Bronfenbrenner, psychologist

A cynical young person is almost the saddest sight to see, because it means that he or she has gone from knowing nothing to believing in nothing.

—Maya Angelou, poet

Respect for the fragility and importance of an individual life is still the first mark of an educated man.

—Norman Cousins, writer

Children have never been very good at listening to their elders, but they have never failed to imitate them.

—James Baldwin, author

The greatest reward I find in teaching
is the hope I feel when students begin to change.

—*Thomas A. Fleming, 1992 National Teacher of the Year*

I believe that the individual who is to be educated is a social individual, and that the society is an organic union of individuals. If we
eliminate the social factor from the child we are left only with an
abstraction; if we eliminate the individual factor from society, we
are left only with an inert and lifeless mass.

—John Dewey, educational philosopher

The Importance of Schools

We cannot wait for a booming economy. We cannot wait for full employment. We cannot wait for the stock market to reach new record highs. Children need us now as their voice and as their champions.

—Dennis Griner, 2004 Washington Teacher of the Year

Enlighten the people generally,
and tyranny and oppressions of body and mind
will vanish like evil spirits at the dawn of day.

—*President Thomas Jefferson*

There is no precedent for the level of violence, drugs, broken homes, child abuse, and crime in today's America. Public education didn't create these problems but deals with them every day.

—Frosty Troy, journalist

There is nothing wrong with America that cannot be cured by what is right with America.

—President William Jefferson Clinton

America's future walks through the doors of our schools each day.

— Mary Jean LeTendre, educator

The American public schools have become the modern-day battleground with the classroom teacher engaged in a vital struggle to bring intellectual enlightenment and cultural enrichment to his students.

—PHILIP BIGLER, 1998 NATIONAL TEACHER OF THE YEAR

I know but one freedom and that is the freedom of the mind.

—Antoine de Saint Exupery, aviator and author

I am proud to be a product of a great American public school. I am proud to be an educator in a great public school.

—JENNIFER J. MONTGOMERY, 2003 NORTH DAKOTA TEACHER OF THE YEAR

Human history becomes more and more a race between education and catastrophe.

—H. G. Wells, author

If we, the American people, government officials, and especially teachers do not boldly and confidently step forward to speak out as well as take action, it will be to the detriment of our children.

—Dennis Griner, 2004 Washington Teacher of the Year

Instead of building more and more prisons, we should be trying to stop the assembly line.

—Merton P. Strommen and Dick Hardel, theologians

Education is the transmission of civilization.

—Will Durant, philosopher

I have seen some of my students being beaten, stabbed, shot at, and sold. But I have also walked hand-in-hand with them as they graduated from high school, attended college, and thrived in the work place. My greatest contributions and accomplishments are reflected in the survival and successes of my students.

—SANDRA L. MCBRAYER, 1994 NATIONAL TEACHER OF THE YEAR

One good teacher in a lifetime may sometimes change
a delinquent into a solid citizen.

—Philip Wylie, writer

Teachers are the last bastion against darkness and ignorance. The intensity of this need was my surprise . . .

—JAMES W. MORRIS, 5TH GRADE TEACHER

Teaching is about being an ambassador for humanity.

—*Lewis Chappelear, 2008 California Teacher of the Year*

Although schools purport to prepare students for a changing world, they are themselves notoriously resistant to change.

—Thomas Hine, writer

It is important that we teach young people how to sit through the discomfort necessary to feel the present moment fully and to stay with a disturbing new idea to examine its source. The pace of our lives and the emphasis on efficiency and multitasking discourage real grappling with issues.

—Vicki Lynn Goldsmith, 2005 Iowa Teacher of the Year

Events in our classrooms today will prompt world events tomorrow.

—J. Lloyd Trump, educator

Among the many purposes of schooling, four stand out to us as having special moral value: to love and care, to serve, to empower and, of course, to learn.

—Andy Hargreaves and Michael Fullan, educators

The principle goal of education is to create men who are capable of doing new things, not simply of repeating what other generations have done—men who are creative, inventive and discoverers.

—JEAN PIAGET, CHILD PSYCHOLOGIST

Education is the guardian genius of democracy. It is the only dictator that free men recognize, and the only ruler that free men require.

—Mirabeau Buonaparte Lamar, politician

If we fail to successfully teach and educate our young people, we are just one generation removed from barbarism.

—*Philip Bigler, 1998 National Teacher of the Year*

The direction in which education starts a man
will determine his future life.

—*Plato, philosopher*

We all need to be a part of the solution-oriented promotion and improvement of public education, not only because it's good for business and the national interest, but because it's good for kids who need to find their way in the world.

—Jennifer J. Montgomery, 2003 North Dakota Teacher of the Year

Whoso neglects learning in his youth, loses the past and is dead to the future.

—*Euripides, playwright*

A teacher can receive no greater reward than the knowledge that he or she helped recover a lost student.

—Anthony J. Mullen, 2009 National Teacher of the Year

The ability to think straight, some knowledge of the past, some vision of the future, some skill to do useful service, some urge to fit that service into the well-being of the community—these are the most vital things education must try to produce.

—Virginia Gildersleeve, educator

There has never been a time when teacher voice and teacher activism were more needed or more important than they are right now.

—Andy Baumgartner, 1999 National Teacher of the Year

The leaps and bounds that our educational system has made in the last one hundred years are very small compared to what we will have to do in the next one hundred years. There is a tidal wave of information and technological change coming that most Americans are unaware of.

—Keil E. Hileman, 2004 Kansas Teacher of the Year

The important achievement of American education in the last thirty years in bringing a much larger proportion of our diverse society into the schools and succeeding with them there to some degree is not adequately recognized in the national debate about school quality. If we could get the youngsters who drop out of high school each year to stay there, it would cause another [test] score decline, and I'd be in favor of it.

—Harold Howe II, U.S. Commissioner of Education

Teaching is what teachers expect to do every day.
—John Goodlad, educator

Surely there is enough for everyone within this country. It is a tragedy that these good things are not more widely shared. All our children ought to be allowed a stake in the enormous richness of America.

—Jonathan Kozol, writer

Liberty cannot be preserved without general knowledge among the people.

— President John Adams

The education and empowerment of women throughout the world cannot fail to result in a more caring, tolerant, just and peaceful life for all.

—Aung San Suu Kyi, human rights activist

But the democratic promise of equal educational opportunity,
half fulfilled, is worse than a promise broken.
It is an ideal betrayed.

—Mortimer J. Adler, educator

We must marshal our political clout on behalf of all children.

—JASON KAMRAS, 2005 NATIONAL TEACHER OF THE YEAR

When I watch news footage of the day we entered school guarded by the 101st soldiers, I am moved by the enormity of that experience. I believe that was a moment when the whole nation took one giant step forward.

—MELBA PATTILLO BEALS, WRITER AND DIVERSITY TRAINER

Not until this century have we undertaken to give twelve years of schooling to all our children . . . Suffrage without schooling produces mobocracy, not democracy—not rule of law, not constitutional government by the people as well as for them.

—Mortimer J. Adler, educator

To refuse to face the task of creating a vision of a future America immeasurably more just and noble and beautiful than the America of today is to evade the most crucial, difficult, and important educational task.

—George S. Counts, educator

It is incompatible with a democracy to train the many and educate the few.

—*Arthur Bestor, historian*

Religious tolerance, mutual respect between vocational groups, belief in the rights of the individual are among the virtues that the best of our high schools now foster.

—*James Bryant Conant, scientist*

I became a teacher because I wanted to help the underdog. Working with immigrants has made me more aware of my ancestor's plight when they came to America for a better life.

—Elizabeth Bowler, ESOL teacher

Few citizens really know what's going on in their schools. They settle for the familiar and ignore the substance.

—*Ted Sizer, educator*

A society of free individuals in which all, through their own work, contribute to the liberation and enrichment of the lives of others, is the only environment in which any individual can really grow normally to his full stature.

—John Dewey, educational philosopher

Information is the currency of democracy.

—*Ralph Nader, social activist*

Freedom to think—which means nothing unless it means freedom to think differently—can be society's most precious gift to itself. The first duty of a school is to defend and cherish it.

—Arthur Bestor, historian

What greater or better gift can we offer the republic than to teach and instruct our youth?

—*Marcus T. Cicero, philosopher*

Public education is the link between our nation and
our dream of liberty and justice for all.

—*Elaine Griffin, 1995 National Teacher of the Year*

There is an old saying that the course of civilization is a race between catastrophe and education. In a democracy such as ours, we must make sure that education wins the race.

—President John F. Kennedy

Upon the education of the people of this country the fate of this country depends.

— Prime Minister Benjamin Disraeli

The most creative and emotionally engaged teachers see themselves not just as educating learners and workers, but as developing citizens.

—Andy Hargreaves and Michael Fullan, educators

The public schools, warts and all, was the single best thing about America. It was the only institution that said to one and all: "Come on! We don't care what color you are or what side of town you live on. Come on!" It was the closest we ever came to the American dream.

—Frosty Troy, journalist

If one accepts the ideal of a democratic, fluid society with a minimum of class distinction, the maximum of fluidity, the maximum of understanding between different vocational groups, then the ideal secondary school is a comprehensive public high school.

—James Bryant Conant, scientist

In an age when science is essential to our safety and to our economic welfare, it might be argued that a shortage of science teachers, and of scientists, is a clear and present danger to the nation.

—James R. Killian, educator

But, because we dared to challenge the Southern tradition
of segregation, this school became, instead,
a furnace that consumed our youth and
forged us into reluctant warriors.

—Melba Pattillo Beals, writer and diversity trainer

Jails and prisons are the complement of schools; so many less as you have of the latter, so many more must you have of the former.

—Horace Mann, educator

Democratic communities help students to be as well as to become.

— Thomas J. Sergiovanni, educator

I regret the trifling narrow contracted education of the females of my own country.

—First Lady Abigail Adams

Every time you stop a school, you will have to build a jail.

—*Mark Twain, author*

As a product of the public education system, I want all American students to have what I had—access to a quality education that enables them to pursue any career they wish, and take on any challenge they choose. Giving our students the best education in the world is a moral imperative and, especially, an economic necessity.

—RICHARD RILEY, U.S. SECRETARY OF EDUCATION

He who opens a school door, closes a prison.

—*Victor Hugo, author*

We must have a program to learn the way out of prison.

—Warren E. Burger, jurist

The benefits of education and of useful knowledge, generally diffused through a community, are essential to the preservation of a free government.

—Sam Houston, politician

Only the educated are free.

—Epictetus, philosopher

Yet even as I wince at the terrible risk we all took, I remember thinking at the time that it was the right decision—because it felt as though the hand of fate was ushering us forward.

—Melba Pattillo Beals, writer and diversity trainer

The highest result of education is tolerance.

—Anne Sullivan (*The Miracle Worker*), educator

The ignorance of one voter in a democracy
impairs the security of all.

—*President John F. Kennedy, at Vanderbilt University (1963)*

A President must call on many persons—some to man the ramparts and to watch the far away, distant posts; others to lead us in science, medicine, education and social progress here at home.

—President Lyndon B. Johnson

Knowledge is the most democratic source of power.

—*Alvin Toffler, writer*

There are obvious places in which government can narrow the chasm between haves and have-nots. One is the public schools, which have been seen as the great leveler, the authentic melting pot.

—Anna Quindlen, writer

The U.S. Bureau of the Census meanwhile sends out printed forms to ask illiterate Americans to indicate their reading levels.

—Jonathan Kozol, writer

The limits of your language are the limits of your world.

—*Ludwig Wittgenstein, philosopher*

Which government is the best? The one that teaches us to govern ourselves.

—Johann Wolfgang von Goethe, philosopher

A good education is like a savings account;
the more you put into it, the richer you are.

—*Anonymous*

If you give me rice, I'll eat today;
if you teach me how to grow rice, I'll eat every day.

—*Mahatma Gandhi, political activist*

I believe in the existence of a great, immortal, immutable principle of natural law, or natural ethics which proves the absolute right to an education of every human being that comes into the world; and which, of course, proves the correlative duty of every government to see that the means of that education are provided for all.

—Horace Mann, educator

He who undertakes to be his own teacher has a fool for a pupil.

—*German proverb*

A child mis-educated is a child lost.

—President John F. Kennedy

Be careful to leave your sons well instructed rather than rich, for the hopes of the instructed are better than the wealth of the ignorant.

—Epictetus, philosopher

The chief cause of human errors is to be found
in the prejudices picked up in childhood.

—*René Descartes, philosopher*

If something offends, don't join others in complaining,
put your brain and muscles to work in fixing the issue and
addressing how it affects the educational environment.

—Eric A. Combs, 2007 Ohio Teacher of the Year

*If a free society cannot help the many who are poor,
it cannot save the few who are rich.*

—President John F. Kennedy

Excellence is the best deterrent to racism or sexism.
—*Oprah Winfrey, multimedia personality*

A little learning, indeed may be a dangerous thing,
but the want of learning is a calamity to any people.

—*Frederick Douglass, writer and abolitionist*

If there is light in the soul/There will be beauty in the person. If there is beauty in the person/There will be harmony in the house. If there is harmony in the house/There will be order in the nation. If there is order in the nation/There will be peace in the world.

—Chinese proverb

A society that is concerned about the strength and wisdom of its culture pays careful attention to its adolescents.

—Ted Sizer, educator

I know no safe depository of the ultimate powers of the society but the people themselves; and if we think them not enlightened enough to exercise their control with a wholesome discretion, the remedy is not to take it from them but to inform their discretion.

—President Thomas Jefferson

The main hope of a nation
lies in the proper education of its youth.

—*Erasmus (Desiderius Erasmus Roterodamus), theologian*

All men by nature desire to know.

—Aristotle, philosopher

I wanted to motivate and inspire the neediest students whom many have written off just because of the circumstances they were born into.

—Kimberly Oliver, 2006 National Teacher of the Year

Upon the subject of education, I can only say that I view it as the most important subject which we as a people may be engaged in.

—President Abraham Lincoln

A good school is the price of peace in the community.
— Ursula Franklin, scientist and educator

The essence of our effort to see that every child has a chance must be to assure each an equal opportunity, not to become equal, but to become different—to realize whatever unique potential of body, mind and spirit he or she possesses.

—John Fischer, writer and singer

We all, whether we know it or not,
are fighting to make the kind of world that we should like.

—Oliver Wendell Holmes, jurist

Education makes people easy to lead, but difficult to drive; easy to govern, but impossible to enslave.

—*Henry Peter Brougham, politician*

Learned Institutions ought to be favorite objects with every free people. They throw that light over the public mind which is the best security against crafty and dangerous encroachments on the public liberty.

——President James Madison

Children don't control the circumstances under which they are born.

—Marion Wright Edelman, social activist

In its education, the soul of a people mirrors itself.

—Richard Haldane, politician

All of us do not have equal talent, but all of us should have an equal opportunity to develop our talents.

—President John F. Kennedy

Teachers are entrusted with the task of creating intelligent, ethical, and productive young adults—a job achieved by understanding the many shades and hues of children and how they learn.

—Anthony J. Mullen, 2009 National Teacher of the Year

The noblest aspect of the American liberal tradition is its respect for diversity.

—Ted Sizer, educator

The public schools are America's children
and require the continuing encouragement, nurture,
and support of America's people.

—Ira Singer, writer

We're a country of inequities, and there are many, many communities all across America where students of particular socioeconomic backgrounds are not being served adequately, quite frankly. I think that one of the most important things we can do as a country is help eliminate these inequities.

—Jason Kamras, 2005 National Teacher of the Year

It takes all sorts to make a world.

—*English proverb*

These students desperately want teachers to colorize their black and white world but are unable to convey their unique needs. Teachers must find the resolve to teach and mentor these fragile students because we represent hope and the promise of a better tomorrow.

—Anthony Mullen, 2009 National Teacher of the Year, describing students with behavioral and emotional disabilities

My teaching philosophy encompasses the whole child. To teach is to cooperatively create a community in which all members are equally valued and all members participate as both teachers and learners.

—Sandra L. McBrayer, 1994 National Teacher of the Year

There are teachers of French and Spanish, Latin and Greek, who have worked for many years without ever seeing the countries whose spirits they have been endeavoring to evoke.

—Gilbert Highet, writer

By providing incentives for master teachers to teach in our schools with the greatest needs, there is hope that our at-risk students will have the single most important resource they need in order to close the achievement gap: quality teachers.

—Kristin Bourguet, 2007 Arizona Teacher of the Year

Parent indifference often rates above low teacher salaries as a cause of dissatisfaction for our nation's teachers.

—Melitta J. Cutright, writer

We must advocate for our students by being a voice for them and communicating their stories of empowerment, resiliency, and success.

—*Thomas R. Smigiel Jr., 2008 Virginia Teacher of the Year*

The most admirable of reforms cannot but fall short in practice if teachers of sufficient quality are not available in sufficient quantity . . . Generally speaking, the more we try to improve our schools, the heavier the teacher's task becomes; and the better our teaching methods, the more difficult they are to apply.

—JEAN PIAGET, CHILD PSYCHOLOGIST

Avoid treating all children equally.

—Lauren K. Ayers, psychologist

Because each child is distinct, it requires an approach
that reminds them of that.

—*Melanie Teemant, 2007 Nevada Teacher of the Year*

**American teachers have a great responsibility. All
children, regardless of background, socioeconomic
status, race or age must be taught to believe that they
can succeed.**

—Sandra L. McBrayer, 1994 National Teacher of the Year

It is our duty to look at our students through the eyes of love,
seeing not who they are today, but what they may become.
We must believe in them so strongly that our belief becomes
contagious—and they catch it. All of them.

—Tamara Steen, 2005 Washington Teacher of the Year

Diversity is paramount because every student brings something
important to each class.

—Susanne H. Frensley, 2007 Tennessee Teacher of the Year

I would express the hope that all American children will be given the opportunity to become literate in their own culture and at the same time develop an international perspective that will enable them to work, lead, and thrive in a global community.

—Mary V. Bicouvaris, 1989 National Teacher of the Year

Sixties' programs were designed to save only the right kids. Only recently have we tried to save them all.

—*Grace Palladino, writer*

Most of my students come from families of modest economic means, but their parents have the same dreams for them as parents everywhere.

—Chauncey Veatch, 2002 National Teacher of the Year

American schools resonate with the diversity of our citizenry. And so, the whole world must be our community.

—*Elaine B. Griffin, 1995 National Teacher of the Year*

Equity to me does not mean that each student receives the same instruction and completes the same task. Rather, I believe equity in a classroom means that each child receives exactly what he or she needs to move forward.

—Kimberly Oliver, 2006 National Teacher of the Year

We can no longer standardize human beings and call it success. We must cherish our differences, abilities, and work to be the very best we can. In this way, we will not leave our country behind.

—Melanie Teemant, 2007 Nevada Teacher of the Year

Education is enriched for all students when learners bring their different experiences, perspectives, and skills to the group.

—Michele Forman, 2001 National Teacher of the Year

On the Lighter Side

The secret of teaching is to appear to have known all your life what you just learned this morning.

—Anonymous

Housework is a breeze. Cooking is a pleasant diversion. Putting up a retaining wall is a lark. But teaching is like climbing a mountain.

—Fawn M. Brodie, biographer

I have often wondered about two things. First, why high-school kids almost invariably hate the books they are assigned to read by their English teachers, and second, why English teachers almost invariably hate the books their students read in their spare time.

—Stephen King, author

If you think your teacher is tough, wait until you get a boss. He doesn't have tenure.

—*Bill Gates, entreprenuer*

My mother tells this story that when I first went to school, I thought I was going to help the teachers. I didn't realize I was going to get educated.

—MOON UNIT ZAPPA, ACTRESS AND MUSICIAN

Adults are obsolete children.

—*Theodor Geisel (Dr. Seuss), children's author and illustrator*

Education seems to be in America the only commodity of which the customer tries to get as little as he can for his money.

—Max Forman, psychiatrist

The difference between stupidity and genius is that genius has its limits.

—**Albert Einstein, physicist**

When I plan lessons, I actively seek to put joy into the event.

—*Margaret Holtschlag, 2000 Michigan Teacher of the Year*

Thank goodness I was never sent to school; it would have rubbed off some of the originality.

—Beatrix Potter, children's author

The price of your hat isn't the measure of your brain.

—*African-American proverb*

His test scores, for general aptitude, showed that he wasn't very apt at anything; he was no natural. This came as no surprise to Garp, who shared with his mother a belief that nothing came naturally.

—JOHN IRVING, AUTHOR

I like a teacher who gives you something to take home to think about besides homework.

—*Lily Tomlin, comedian*

If I were asked to enumerate ten educational stupidities, the giving of grades would head the list . . . If I can't give a child a better reason for studying than a grade on a report card, I ought to lock my desk and go home and stay there.

—Dorothy De Zouche, educator

Education costs money, but so does ignorance.
—*Sir Claude Moser*

Shortchange your education now and you may be short of change the rest of your life.

—Anonymous

Anyone who stops learning is old, whether twenty or eighty. Anyone who keeps learning today is young. The greatest thing in life is to keep your mind young.

—Henry Ford, entreprenuer

The sound that best describes teaching is the sound of a car being driven by someone just learning how to drive a stick shift. It's getting somewhere, but nowhere quickly, and there are a lot of stops and starts in between.

—Margaret Struhar, English teacher

The man who graduates today and stops learning tomorrow is uneducated the day after.

—Newton D. Baker, politician

Few statements on quality education deal with teachers' needs in day-to-day school operation. Teachers, apparently, are taken for granted as a part of the classroom scenery, like desks, chairs, and books.

—J. LLOYD TRUMP, EDUCATOR

Education is when you read the fine print.
Experience is what you get if you don't.

—*Pete Seeger, musician*

Life is a festival only to the wise.
—*Ralph Waldo Emerson, philosopher*

Parents may tell/But never teach/Unless they practice/ What they preach.

—Anonymous

Analysts of the American psyche may explain that we pick particularly on the schools when we're unhappy with ourselves . . .

—Ted Sizer, educator

Be wiser than other people if you can; but do not tell them so.

—Lord Chesterfield (Philip Stanhope), politician

It is best for the wise man not to seem wise.

—Aeschylus, playwright

If you see two children, one of whom is clean and the other is dirty, you tend to suppose that the clean one's parents have a larger income than the parent's of the dirty one. Consequently snobs try to keep their children very clean. This is an abominable tyranny which interferes with the children doing a great many of the things they had better be doing.

—Bertrand Russell, philosopher

Love truth, but pardon error.

—Volatire (François-Marie Arouet), philosopher

If nobody said anything unless he knew what he was talking about, a ghastly hush would descend upon the earth.

—Alan Patrick Herbert, writer and politician

Just think of the tragedy of teaching children not to doubt.

—Clarence Darrow, defense attorney

There are two ways to slide easily through life: to believe everything or to doubt everything. Both ways save us from thinking.

—ALFRED KORZYBSKI, PHILOSOPHER

Wisdom is as the moon rises,
perceptible not in progress but in result.

—Chinese proverb

Education is . . . hanging around until you've caught on.

—Robert Frost, poet

One of the greatest problems of our time is that many are schooled but few are educated.

—Thomas Moore, poet and entertainer

The mind is more vulnerable than the stomach, because it can be poisoned without feeling immediate pain.

—Helen MacInnes, author

When you stack up the years we are allowed against all there is to read, time is very short indeed.

—*Stephen King, author*

Men dress their children's minds as they do their bodies, in the prevailing fashion.

—Herbert Spencer, philosopher

I am afraid we must make the world honest before we can honestly say to our children that honesty is the best policy.

—George Bernard Shaw, playwright

You can pay people to teach, but you can't pay them to care.

—Marva Collins, educator

Everyone is ignorant, only on different subjects.
— Will Rogers, entertainer

How is it that little children are so intelligent and men so stupid? It must be education that does it.

—Alexandre Dumas, writer

It is bad enough to see young fools, but worse to see old fools.

—BRIGHAM YOUNG, THEOLOGIAN

Quite frankly, teachers are the only profession that teach our children.

—Vice President Dan Quayle

He was so learned that he could name a horse in nine languages; so ignorant that he bought a cow to ride on.

—BENJAMIN FRANKLIN, AUTHOR AND PRINTER

Our metaphors arise from the factory floor and issue from the military manual. Education, apparently, is something someone does to somebody else.

—Ted Sizer, educator

It is better to ask some of the questions than know all of the answers.

—*James Thurber, author*

We have inadvertently designed a system in which being good at what you do as a teacher is not formally rewarded, while being poor at what you do is seldom corrected nor penalized.

—Elliot Eisner, educator

He who is ashamed of asking is ashamed of learning.
—*Danish proverb*

I was gratified to be able to answer promptly.
I said I didn't know.

—*Mark Twain, author*

It is indeed ironic that we spend our school days yearning to graduate and our remaining days waxing nostalgic about our school days.

—Isabel Waxman

A gifted teacher is as rare as a gifted doctor, and makes far less money.

—ANONYMOUS

Teaching is not a lost art, but the regard for it is a lost tradition.

—Jacques Barzun, writer

In the school I went to, they asked a kid to prove the law of gravity and he threw the teacher out of the window.

—RODNEY DANGERFIELD, COMEDIAN

Anyone who refuses to speak out off campus does not deserve to be listened to on campus.

—Theodore M. Hesburgh, theologian and educator

Ignorant people in preppy clothes are more dangerous to America than oil embargoes.

—V. S. Naipaul, author

For God's sake give me the young man who has brains enough to make a fool of himself!

—Robert Louis Stevenson, author

Experience is the worst teacher;
it gives the test before presenting the lesson.

—*Vernon Law, baseball player*

Winter is the time for study, you know, and the colder it is the more studious we are.

—HENRY DAVID THOREAU, WRITER AND NATURALIST

Wit is educated insolence.

—*Aristotle, philosopher*

Microscopes and telescopes really confuse our minds.
—*Johann Wolfgang von Goethe, philosopher*

I would be most content if my children grew up to be the kind of people who think decorating consists mostly of building enough bookshelves.

—ANNA QUINDLEN, WRITER

Children seldom misquote you.
In fact, they usually repeat word for word
what you shouldn't have said.

—*Anonymous*

I think a secure profession for young people is history, because in the future, there will be so much more of it to teach.

—Bill Muse, writer

When a teacher calls a boy by his entire name, it means trouble.

—Mark Twain, author

A professor is one who talks in someone else's sleep.

—W. H. Auden, poet

I have never been jealous. Not even when my dad finished fifth grade a year before I did.

—Jeff Foxworthy, comedian

Remember in elementary school you were told that in case of fire you have to line up quietly in a single file from smallest to tallest? What is the logic in that? What, do tall people burn slower?

—Warren Hutcherson, writer

I took a test in Existentialism. I left all the answers blank and got 100.

—WOODY ALLEN, ENTERTAINER

I'm not going to buy my kids an encyclopedia.
Let them walk to school like I did.

—*Yogi Berra, baseball player*

My father wanted me to have all the educational opportunities he never had, so he sent me to a girls school.

—Jack Herbert, artist

My school colors were clear. We used to say, "I'm not naked, I'm in the band."

—**Stephen Wright, comedian**

It's like being grounded for 18 years.
—A New York City Board of Education poster
warning against teen pregnancy (1986)

My school days were the happiest days of my life; which should give you some indication of the misery I've endured over the past twenty-five years.

—Paul Merton, entertainer

In the first place, God made idiots. That was for practice. Then he made school boards.

—MARK TWAIN, AUTHOR

We all learn by experience
but some of us have to go to summer school.

—Peter De Vries, author

But there are advantages to being elected President. The day after I was elected, I had my high school grades classified Top Secret.

—President Ronald Reagan

In grade school I was smart, but I didn't have any friends. In high school, I quit being smart and started having friends.

—David Spade, comedian

There is nothing so stupid as the educated man if you get him off the thing he was educated in.

—Will Rogers, entertainer

True terror is to wake up one morning and discover that your high school class is running the country.

—*Kurt Vonnegut Jr., author*

Smartness runs in my family. When I went to school I was so smart my teacher was in my class for five years.

—Gracie Allen, comedian

You know how to tell if the teacher is hung over? Movie Day.

—Jay Mohr, comedian

As long as teachers give tests,
there will always be prayer in schools.

—Anonymous

It is nobler to be good, and it is nobler to teach others to be good—and less trouble!

—MARK TWAIN, AUTHOR

I never did very well in math—
I could never seem to persuade the teacher that
I hadn't meant my answers literally.

—*Calvin Trillin, writer*

My education was dismal. I went to a series of schools for mentally disturbed teachers.

—Woody Allen, entertainer

If the teacher said on the report card, This kid is a total and hopeless jackass who may have trouble learning his zip code, then the parent wouldn't be teased by the possibility of scholastic success.

—Bill Cosby, comedian

Time is a great teacher, but unfortunately it kills all its pupils.

—Louis Hector Berlioz, composer

Equality is not when a female Einstein gets promoted to assistant professor. Equality is when a female schlemiel moves ahead as fast as a male schlemiel.

—EWALD B. NYQUIST, EDUCATOR

I think I am, therefore, I am. I think.

—George Carlin, comedian

Why are there five syllables in the word "monosyllabic"? And how come abbreviated is such a long word?

—Steven Wright, comedian

Is sloppiness in speech caused by ignorance or apathy? I don't know and I don't care.

—William Safire, journalist and speech writer

In America the young are always ready to give to
those who are older than themselves the
full benefits of their inexperience.

—*Oscar Wilde, playwright*

**My father must have had some elementary education for
he could read and write and keep accounts inaccurately.**

—George Bernard Shaw, playwright

Whenever you asked him how he was doing in school, he always
said, "No problem." And his answer made sense: there was no
problem, no confusion about how he was doing. He had failed
everything; and what he hadn't failed, he hadn't taken yet.

—Bill Cosby, comedian

*Television commercials are educational. They teach you
how stupid advertisers think you are.*

—Anonymous

SUGGESTED BUMPER STICKER: We Are the Proud Parents of a Child Whose Self-Esteem Is Sufficient that He Doesn't Need Us Advertising His Minor Scholastic Achievement on the Bumper of Our Car.

—George Carlin, comedian

Teachers are sometimes thought of as respectable drudges—like hospital nurses, or even like attendants in an asylum for the harmless insane.

—GILBERT HIGHET, WRITER

You can lead a boy to college, but you cannot make him think.

—*Elbert Hubbard, writer*

I was thrown out of NYU my freshman year . . . for cheating on my metaphysics final. You know, I looked within the soul of the boy sitting next to me.

—Woody Allen, entertainer

If ignorance is bliss,
there should be more happy people.

—*Victor Cousins, philosopher*

When you think about it, attention deficit disorder makes a lot of sense. In this country there isn't a lot worth paying attention to.

—George Carlin, comedian

I have never let my schooling interfere with my education.

—Mark Twain, author

If there were no schools to take the children away from home part of the time, the insane asylum would be filled with mothers.

—Edgar Watson Howe, writer

The vanity of teaching often tempteth a man to forget he is a blockhead.

—George Savile, politician

Whose cruel idea was it for the word "lisp" to have an "s" in it?

—Steven Wright, comedian

Garp knew what to take for courses and whom to have for teachers. That is often the difference between doing well or poorly in a school. He was not really a gifted student, but he had direction.

—JOHN IRVING, AUTHOR

Praise does wonders for our sense of hearing.

—Arnold H. Glasgow, psychologist

Teaching for tests creates learnoids.

—Alan Scott Winston

Compromise is fine for people who aren't as right as me.

—ESMÉ RAJI CODELL, EDUCATOR

Start a program for gifted children,
and every parent demands that his child be enrolled.

—*Thomas Bailey, historian*

If you promise not to believe everything your child says happens at this school, I'll promise not to believe everything he says happens at home.

—A note to students' parents from an English schoolmaster as quoted in the *Wall Street Journal* (1985)

As for helping me in the outside world, the Convent taught me only that if you spit on a pencil eraser, it will erase ink.

—Dorothy Parker, writer

The only reason I always try to meet and know the parents better is because it helps me to forgive their children.

—Louis Johannot, educator

A fellow declaring he's no fool usually has his suspicions.

—Wilson Mizner, playwright

The University of Miami is not a campus with visible school spirit, just visible tan lines.

—Lisa Birnbach, writer

I won't say ours was a tough school, but we had our own coroner. We used to write essays like: What I'm going to be if I grow up.

—LENNY BRUCE, COMEDIAN

They wanted a great university without building a great university. They knew a lot about football, but not a lot about academia.

—Brad Carter, educator, on the NCAA's suspension of Southern Methodist University's football program

Knowledge is good.

—Emil Faber, fictional founder of Faber College, from the film Animal House

Minerva House . . . was "a finishing establishment for young ladies," where some twenty girls of the ages from thirteen to nineteen inclusive, acquired a smattering of everything and a knowledge of nothing.

—Charles Dickens, author

What we want is to see the child in pursuit of knowledge, and not knowledge in pursuit of the child.

—GEORGE BERNARD SHAW, PLAYWRIGHT

Closure to the Lesson

What rewards do you find in teaching? What rewards don't I find in teaching?

—Daniel R. Kuznik, 2008 Indiana Teacher of the Year

Education is the best provision for old age.

—*Aristotle, philosopher*

There is no real teacher who in practice does not believe in the existence of the soul, or in a magic that acts on it through speech.

—Allan Bloom, philosopher

Education breeds confidence. Confidence breeds hope. Hope breeds peace.

—Confucius, philosopher

The best teachers give their pupils both a sense of order, discipline, control; and a powerful stimulus which urges them to take their destinies in their own hands, kick over rules, and transgress all boundaries.

—GILBERT HIGHET, WRITER

They can because they think they can.
—Virgil (Publius Vergilius Maro), poet

Teaching is leaving a vestige of one self in the development of another. And surely the student is a bank where you can deposit your most precious treasures.

—Eugene P. Bertin, textbook author

My heart is singing for joy . . . The light of understanding
has shone in my little pupil's mind, and behold,
all things are changed.

—*Anne Sullivan (*The Miracle Worker*), educator*

We need to bring dignity back and
realize we're doing the most noble of professions.

—*Laurie R. Carlton, 2008 Louisiana Teacher of the Year*

Language is a living, kicking, growing, flitting, evolving reality, and the teacher should spontaneously reflect its vibrant and protean qualities.

—John A. Rassias, educator

Education is not to reform students or amuse them or to make them expert technicians. It is to unsettle their minds, widen their horizons, inflame their intellects, teach them to think straight, if possible.

—Robert M. Hutchins, educator

Teaching is the most inherently hopeful act that I know of.

—Patricia Murphy, educator

The difference between school and life? In school, you're taught a lesson and then given a test. In life, you're given a test that teaches you a lesson.

—Tom Bodett, entertainer

The mind is not a vessel to be filled, but a fire to be ignited.

—Plutarch (Lucius Mestrius Plutarchus), biographer

The teacher is one who makes two ideas grow where only one grew before.

—Elbert Hubbard, writer

A teacher affects eternity;
he can never tell where his influence stops.

—*Henry Adams, writer*

Education happens when hope exceeds expectation.

—Andy Hargreaves and Michael Fullan, educators

You can get help from teachers, but you are going to have to learn a lot by yourself, sitting alone in a room.

—Theodor Geisel (Dr. Seuss), children's author and illustrator

I put the relation of a fine teacher to a student just below the relation of a mother to a son . . .

— Thomas Wolfe, author

Whoever teaches his son teaches not alone his son but also his son`s son, and so on to the end of generations

—Hebrew proverb

Our modern world owes a great deal of thanks to schools and teachers; we are the beneficiaries of their noble adventure.

—Anthony Mullen, 2009 National Teacher of the Year

I do not teach children, I give them joy.

—*Isadora Duncan, dancer*

When the uncapped potential of a student meets the liberating art of a teacher, a miracle unfolds.

—Mary Hatwood Futrell, educator

Teacher appreciation makes the world of education go around.

—Helen Peters, writer

It is a profession based on optimism, on knowing that life and work can always be improved and made better, and we work with students who are continually looking toward the future. What could be more happy, more inspiring than that?

—Steve Gardiner, 2008 Montana Teacher of the Year

Life is amazing: and the teacher had better prepare himself to be a medium for that amazement.

—Edward Blishen, author

I really believe in what I'm doing.

—*Mitsuye Conover, 2000 Oklahoma Teacher of the Year*

None of us got where we are solely by pulling ourselves up by our bootstraps. We got here because somebody—a parent, a teacher, an Ivy League crony or a few nuns—bent down and helped us pick up our boots.

—THURGOOD MARSHALL, JURIST

I am not embarrassed to vocalize the positive qualities of my profession, nor am I slow to defend it. It is not myself that I seek to champion, but the good that teachers do.

—Rae Ellen McKee, 1991 National Teacher of the Year

Wrap the student around the curriculum,
not the curriculum around the student.

—*George Edwin Goodfellow, 2008 Rhode Island Teacher of the Year*

Teaching kids to count is fine,
but teaching them what counts is best.

—*Bob Talbert, writer*

**There's no greater happiness than being able to lift other
people, to be able to serve and lift other people.**

—Hal W. Adams, 2008 Utah Teacher of the Year

Teaching is the greatest act of optimism.

—Colleen Wilcox, educator

**Choose a job you love, and you will never have to work a
day in your life.**

—Confucius, philosopher

Seek knowledge from the cradle to the grave.

—*Muhammad, theologian*

A truly good book teaches me better than to read it. I must soon lay it down, and commence living on its hint. What I began by reading, I must finish by acting.

—HENRY DAVID THOREAU, WRITER AND NATURALIST

Try to learn something about everything
and everything about something.

—*Thomas Huxley, biologist*

Work 'em hard, play 'em hard, feed 'em up to the nines and send 'em to bed so tired that they are asleep before their heads are on the pillow.

—Frank L. Boyden, educator

Keep on sowing your seed, for you never know which will grow—perhaps it all will.

—Ecclesiastes

I am only one, but still I am one. I cannot do everything, but still I can do something; and because I cannot do everything I will not refuse to do the something that I can do.

—Edward Everett Hale, author

And in the end/the love you take/
is equal to/the love you make.

—*Paul McCartney, singer/songwriter*

Carpe diem, seize the day boys, make your lives extraordinary.

—Robin Williams as teacher John Keating in the film *Dead Poets Society*

Our dreams act as compasses, illuminating the direction we should travel as we set a course of action for our lives. A dream gives us hope for the future and a vision for the present.

—Jason Scott Fulmer, 2004 South Carolina Teacher of the Year

No act of kindness, no matter how small, is ever wasted.

—*Aesop, storyteller*

Nurture your minds with great thoughts. To believe in the heroic makes heroes.

—Prime Minister Benjamin Disraeli

As your body grows bigger/Your mind must flower/
It's great to learn/'cause knowledge is power!

—*Tom Yohe, children's songwriter*

The future is yet full of trial and success. There is happiness to be enjoyed! There is good to be done! Exchange this false life of thine for a true one.

—Nathaniel Hawthorne, author

The circumstances that surround a man's life are not important. How that man responds to those circumstances is important. His response is the ultimate determining factor between success and failure.

—Booker T. Washington, educator

If you rest, you rust.

—Helen Hayes, actress

Life isn't about finding yourself.
Life is about creating yourself.

—George Bernard Shaw, playwright

We are the inheritors of a past that gives us every reason to believe that we will succeed.

—A Nation at Risk (1983)

You don't have to be tall to see the moon.

—African proverb

Education is the power to think clearly, the power to act well in the world's work, and the power to appreciate life.

—Brigham Young, theologian

Knowledge is not simply another commodity. On the contrary. Knowledge is never used up. It increases by diffusion and grows by dispersion.

—Daniel J. Boorstin, writer

You always pass failure on the road to success.

—Mickey Rooney, actor

Genius is one percent inspiration, ninety-nine percent perspiration.

—Thomas A. Edison, inventor

Life is ten percent what happens to me and ninety percent how I react to it.

—Charles Swindoll, theologian

I don't know what your destiny will be, but one thing I know: the only ones among you who will be truly happy are those who will have sought and found how to serve.

—ALBERT SCHWEITZER, PHYSICIAN AND THEOLOGIAN

When the One Great Scorer comes to write against your name/He marks not that you won or lost/But how you played the game.

—Grantland Rice, sports journalist

Nurture your mind with great thoughts, for you will never go any higher than you think.

—Prime Minister Benjamin Disraeli

If you want to increase your success rate,
double your failure rate.

—*Thomas Watson Sr., corporate executive*

**Yesterday is a dream, tomorrow but a vision. But today
well lived makes every yesterday a dream of happiness,
and every tomorrow a vision of hope. Look well, therefore,
to this day.**

—Sanskrit proverb

*Make a true estimate of your own ability,
then raise it ten percent.*

—Norman Vincent Peale, theologian

It is good even for old men to learn wisdom.

—Aeschylus, playwright

When you do a thing, do it with all your might. Put your whole soul into it. Stamp it with your own personality . . . Nothing great was ever achieved without enthusiasm.

—Ralph Waldo Emerson, philosopher

Knowledge is the eye of desire and can become the pilot of the soul.

—Will Durant, philosopher

Reflect upon your present blessings, of which every man has plenty; not on your past misfortunes, of which all men have some.

—Charles Dickens, author

The great tragedy of life doesn't lie in failing to reach your goals. The great tragedy lies in having no goals to reach.

—Benjamin E. Mays, educator

We must accept finite disappointment, but we must never lose infinite hope.

—Martin Luther King Jr., theologian and political activist

Strength does not come from physical capacity.
It comes from an indomitable will.

—*Mahatma Gandhi, political activist*

I am only one; but still I am one. I cannot do everything, but still I can do something. I will not refuse to do the something I can do.

—Helen Keller, author and lecturer

Wherever you go, no matter what the weather, always bring your own sunshine.
—*Anthony J. D'Angelo, writer*

The larger the island of knowledge, the longer the shoreline of wonder.

—Ralph W. Sockman, theologian

You can't live a perfect day without doing something for someone who will never be able to repay you.

—John Wooden, basketball coach

The true meaning of life, Wesley, is to plant trees under whose shade you do not expect to sit.

—Nelson Henderson, pioneer, in a graduation day message to is son

Even if I knew that tomorrow the world would go to pieces, I would still plant my apple tree.

—Martin Luther, theologian

Imagination is more important than knowledge.

—ALBERT EINSTEIN, PHYSICIST

I know of no more encouraging fact than the unquestionable ability of man to elevate his life by conscious endeavor.

—Henry David Thoreau, writer and naturalist

Anything one man can imagine,
other men can make real.

—*Jules Verne, author*

What lies behind us and what lies before us are tiny matters compared to what lies within us.

—Oliver Wendell Holmes, jurist

I respect faith, but doubt is what gets you an education.

—Wilson Mizner, playwright

When love and skill work together,
expect a masterpiece.

—*John Ruskin, art critic and social theorist*

As long as you live, keep learning how to live.
— Seneca, philosopher

Employ your time in improving yourself by other men's writings, so that you shall gain easily what others have labored hard for.

—Socrates, philosopher

Excellence can be achieved if we . . . care more than others think is wise. Risk more than others think is safe. Dream more than others think is practical. Expect more than others think is possible.

—COMET HILL PRIMARY SCHOOL (VICTORIA, AUSTRALIA) MISSION STATEMENT

No matter what accomplishments you achieve, somebody helped you.

—**Althea Gibson, tennis player**

If you can dream it, you can do it.

—*Walt Disney, animator*

From what we get, we can make a living; what we give, however, makes a life.

—Arthur Ashe, tennis player

Don't judge each day by the harvest you reap, but by the seeds you plant.

—*Robert Louis Stevenson, author*

Far and away the best prize that life offers is the chance to work hard at work worth doing.

—President Theodore Roosevelt

The very least you can do in your life is to figure out what you hope for. And the most you can do is live inside that hope. Not admire it from a distance but live right in it, under its roof.

—Barbara Kingsolver, author

I love to see a young girl go out and grab the world by the lapels.

—*Maya Angelou, poet*

All growth is a leap in the dark.

—*Henry Miller, author*

Talent builds itself in stillness,
character in the stream of the world.

—*Johann Wolfgang von Goethe, philosopher*

—Sometimes one man with courage is a majority.

President Andrew Jackson

It's easy to make a buck. It's a lot tougher to make a difference.

—Tom Brokaw, broadcaster

Many great actions are committed in small struggles.

—Victor Hugo, author

Only the mind cannot be sent into exile.

—Ovid (Publius Ovidius Naso), poet

We may have all come on different ships, but we're in the same boat now.

—Martin Luther King Jr., theologian and political activist

I see rainbows where others see only rain.

—Sharon M. Draper, 1997
National Teacher of the Year

To dream is to be filled with hope. I know this because I see the faces of hope daily.

—CHAUNCEY VEATCH, 2002 NATIONAL TEACHER OF THE YEAR

When inspiration does not come to me,
I go half way to meet it.

—Sigmund Freud, psychologist

Bibliography

Adler, Mortimer J. *The Paideia Proposal: An Educational Manifesto*. New York: MacMillan Publishing Co., 1982.

Albom, Mitch. *Tuesdays with Morrie*. New York: Doubleday, 1997.

Andrews, Robert, Mary Biggs, and Michael Seidel et al. *The Columbia Encyclopedia*. Sixth Edition. New York: Columbia University Press, 2001.

Archambault, Regina D. *John Dewey, Educational Philosopher on Education*. Chicago: The University of Chicago Press, 1964.

Baruch, Bernard. *Baruch: My Own Story*. New York: Henry Holt & Co, 1996.

Beals, Melba Patillo. *Warriors Don't Cry*. New York: Washington Square Press, 1994.

Bloom, Harold. *Stories and Poems for Extremely Intelligent Children of All Ages*. New York: Scribner, 2001.

Bok, Derek. *Universities and the Future of America*. Durham, N.C.: Duke University Press, 1990.

Boorstin, Daniel. The Image: *A Guide to Pseudo-Events in America*. New York: Colophon Books, 1961.

Carlin, George. *Napalm and Silly Putty*. New York: Hyperion, 2001.

Codell, Esmé Raji. *Educating Esmé: Diary of a Teacher's First Year*. Chapel Hill, N.C.: Algonquin Books, 1999.

Cosby, Bill. *Fatherhood*. Garden City, New York: Doubleday & Company, Inc., 1986.

Cutright, Melitta J. *The National PTA Talks to Parents: How to Get the Best Education for Your Child*. New York: Doubleday, 1989.

Dewey, John. *Philosophy of Education*. Totowa, N.J.: Littlefield, Adams & Co., 1958.

Gibran, Kahlil. *The Prophet*. New York: Alfred A. Knopf, 1973.

Goethe, Johann Wolfgang von. *Maxims and Reflections*. London: Penguin Classics, 1998.

Gross, Beatrice and Ronald Gross. *The Great School Debate: Which Way for American Education*. New York: Simon & Schuster, Inc., 1985.

Gross, Ronald. *The Teacher and the Taught*. New York: Dell Publishing Co., 1963.

Hargreaves, Andy, and Michael Fullan. *What's Worth Fighting for Out There?* New York: Teachers College Press, 1998.

Hegel, Georg. *Elements of the Philosophy of Right*. Berlin: University of Berlin, 1821.

Highet, Gilbert. *The Immortal Profession*. New York: Weybright and Talley, 1976.

hooks, bell. *Teaching to Transgress: Education as the Practice of Freedom*. London: Routledge, 1994.

Iacocca, Lee A. *Iacocca*. New York: Bantam Books, 1986.

Kozol, Jonathan. *Illiterate America*. Garden City, N.Y.: Anchor Press/ Doubleday, 1985.

Kozol, Jonathan. *Savage Inequalities: Children in America's Schools*. New York: Crown Publishers, 1991.

Lillard, Paula Polk. *Montessori Today: A Comprehensive Approach to Education from Birth to Adulthood.* New York: Shocken Books, 1996.

Piaget, Jean. *Science of Education and the Psychology of the Child.* New York: Orion Press, 1970.

Pusey, Nathan M. *The Age of the Scholar.* Boston: Harvard University Press, 1963.

Salinger, J. D. *The Catcher in the Rye.* New York: Little, Brown and Company, 1951.

Sergiovanni, Thomas J. *Building Community in Schools.* San Francisco: Jossey-Bass Inc., 1994.

Shopenhauer, Arthur, and E. F. J. Payne (editor). *Parerga and Paralipomena: Volume 1: Six Long Philosophical Essays.* New York: Oxford University Press, 2001.

Simpson, James B. *Simpson's Contemporary Quotations.* Boston: Houghton Mifflin Company, 1988.

Sizer, Ted. *Horace's Compromise.* Boston: Houghton Mifflin, 1984.

Sizer, Ted. *Places for Learning, Places for Joy: Speculations on American School Reform.* Cambridge, Mass., 1973.

Tate, Claudia (editor). *Black Women Writers at Work.* New York: Continuum, 1983.

Toffler, Alvin. *Powershift: Knowledge, Wealth, and Violence at the Edge of the 21st Century.* New York: Bantam, 1990.

Whitehead, Alfred North. *Aims of Education and Other Essays.* New York: New American Library, 1958.

About the Author

Randy Howe is a special education teacher in New Haven and has written or edited more than twenty books, including *Teacher Haiku, The Quotable Teacher, Flags of the Fifty States: Their Colorful Histories and Significance,* and *A+ Educators*. He lives in Connecticut with his wife and two children.